MY LIFE IN A SILENT STRUGGLE

QUINTION LITTLE

ISBN 978-1-312-55819-9

Acknowledgments

First and foremost I would like to thank my Heavenly Father for keeping me during my 20 year journey/test. Next, I would like to thank my mother, Linda Little, for being by my side every step of the way. Last, but not least, I would like to thank my support team. You know who you are. If you have ever taken care of me, checked on me, visited me in the hospital, called, text, or sent up a prayer, THANK YOU THANK YOU THANK YOU!!

TABLE OF CONTENTS

MY LIFE IN A SILENT STRUGGLE 1
INTRODUCTION 5
Chapter 1 (1993) 21
Chapter 2 (2001) 27
Chapter 3 (2002) 37
Chapter 4 (2003) 51
Chapter 5 (2004) 57
Chapter 6 (2007) 63
Chapter 7 (2008) 69
Chapter 8 (2009) 73
Chapter 9 (2010) 77
Chapter 10 (2011) 81
Chapter 11 (2012) 89

INTRODUCTION

Finding out about my disease was a shock for me and my family. Before I was diagnosed with Type 1 Diabetes, I knew nothing of the illness. As a matter of fact, I've never even heard the name diabetes before. That would soon change. I found out about my disease at the age of 9. This is when I was diagnosed with juvenile diabetes. I got more reaction out of my mother during this time. She was a single mother raising 6 children. I was the second oldest, first son but I had established myself as the rock of our family. When I became ill, my mother was at a loss for words, sad and depressed but yet she held on to her faith during this situation. Something of this magnitude was new for her because this wasn't like getting the common cold. To this day, I've never asked my mother if she knew anything about diabetes before I was diagnosed. Whether she did or didn't, I could tell the differences because she was a pro when it came down to taking care of me but, I guess that's just a mother's job. With me being diagnosed at age 9, my siblings were just as young as I was; except my oldest sister who was 12. We all didn't know or understand what was happening to me, but their reaction showed a great deal of sadness and pain. They didn't understand what my life's journey was about to be over the next "x" amount of years. As siblings, we did everything together but this disease had a hold on my childhood.

I would characterize my childhood as a great one before and after my illness came into my life. I was a young boy who was full of energy that LOVED life!!! Granted that I was happier before being diagnosed with type 1 diabetes but life is life, what can you do when you're hit with such obstacles? I was never a troubled child in school. I was an honor student since day one. I was very friendly to everybody around me and that's how I made some long lasting friendships that I still have today from my childhood. I was just a likeable guy. A lot of my childhood friends knew in great detail about my illness and could help me at any given moment when needed. I was still able to function throughout my childhood like the normal kids/teenagers around me but with a little more caution. As I got into Jr. High School and High School and was able to play sports, I did. I played football and ran track. I didn't have the energy most kids had at our age to play sports at the peak of their life. With type 1 diabetes, I had to watch the amount of energy I used when practicing and playing in games, because, if my blood sugar dropped too low from using too much energy, I could go into a coma. So playing sports became very tricky. I would have to have sweets with me at all time, because exercising drops the sugar level in my body. Even though I knew this, I still wanted to be a normal kid like everybody else. Those childhood friends/friendships that I've made over 20 something years ago, I wouldn't trade them for nothing in the world. If you're reading this, you know who you are- so Thank You from deep down in the bottom of my heart. You have helped me along the way of my journey and for that I am forever grateful. True friends are hard to come by...

One of my most joyous events is when I got the chance to stay weekends with my grandmother on my father's side of the family. I loved going there and doing things with my grandfather. He was a great guy that did a lot of hands on work and took me around when he did odd jobs. My aunt was a school teacher so when she had time away from doing her lesson plan, we would play my favorite board game "Sorry". Another joyous event came when I was enrolled to go to Camp Alders gate in Little Rock, AR to be around other kids with juvenile diabetes. Here, I was able to learn more about my illness while learning from those who have been living with it longer than me, all while having the time of my life. But my most joyous event(s) came when I wasn't being sick from my diabetes. It may not seem like much to most but for me, not being sick for a day or two gave me such joy.

My 1st dramatic event from my childhood would be when I went into a coma for 2 weeks. This was the time we found out I was a type 1 diabetic with a blood sugar over 1400+. For 2 weeks my mother stayed in the chapel praying for God to return me to her and that she would promise to take care of me. She kept her word and has been by my side every step of the way. Another dramatic journey was when I started getting into cooking to remove my focus off of being sick. I was 10 years old and I was frying chicken wings, (my favorite protein by the way), and I had taken my medicine for the day but hadn't eaten anything to balance out the insulin. The next thing I remember was waking up at the hospital with tubes inside of me. I was told I had passed out because my blood sugar had dropped too low. Other occurrences were just being in and out of the hospital the first two years, every other month, for 2-3 weeks out of the month. This was no way for a kid to spend his time growing up.

I don't have the best relationship with my father, but my mother is a different story. My mother was a strong woman when I was growing up and still is today. She was taking care of her six kids by herself. She would work 2 and 3 jobs to make sure we had a roof over our head, clothes on our backs and food to eat. She never really complained about life and life's problems. She just kept her head lifted high and prayed to God for blessings upon blessings, and he answered. She's smart, beautiful, driven, God-fearing, outgoing, great personality and loving. They say you only get one mom and I'm truly blessed to have Linda "Penny" Little as my mother!!!

My immediate family consists of my mother and my 5 siblings. My mother, Linda Little, most call her Penny, is the heart and soul of this family. She is currently unable to work due to medical issues. My oldest sister, Candi Cook, has given me two nieces and one nephew. She is a stay at home mom. My sister, Danielle Hair, has given me three nephews and two nieces. She is currently a supervisor at UALR in the Food Court. My next sister, Evonne Hair, has finished her Associates degree in Business and currently works for UALR Events/Food Court. She looks forward to getting her Bachelor's degree one day as well. She doesn't have any kids. My brother, Le'Vorn Hair has given me a niece, as well. He is currently in Georgia working. My baby sister, Sha Perry is an overnight stocker at Wal-Mart. She doesn't have any kids either. These are six people that I hold near and dear to my heart, along with my nieces and nephews, as well as, my daughter Diamond Little.

I've had some fun and exciting times in my teenage years. By this stage in my life, I had learned to control my illness and not let it take control of me. Now don't get me wrong, I still had episodes that would cause me to be in the hospital, but not like they were in my childhood. I was able to get a job my 10th grade year in high school. I was also sophomore of the Year for the state of Arkansas in high school. I was crowned Prom King my senior year in high school. I took a lot of interesting trips out of town to have fun with family and friends, while not letting my diabetes prevent me from doing so. I was having just as much fun as any normal teenager was having.

I was a magnet that was drawn to the opposite sex!!! Once I got of age where I was really into girls, it was no turning back. I've had countless relationships, some good and some bad. I take nothing away from the bad relationships, because most of them were my fault in the end. I was still in my playa mode and I just kept playing the field up until it backfired on my and I was truly hurt. I've learned from each and every one of them. You must understand that my confidence in speaking to any female was at 1000 on a scale of 1-10. I knew conversation was key and since I could hold a conversation with a female on any level about any subject, I was always winning. Women like a man that has great conversation, but more importantly, a great listener. Besides, my conversation with women, did I mention I can cook? Cooking was another exceptional way that I was able to relate to women and get them to like me. I kept many other tricks and trades in my possession to charm the ladies, like my personal grooming and my personality. I considered myself as a triple threat type of guy, great conversationalist, great listener and handsome...

As stated already, I've had countless of relationships, but I am one to believe in karma, as well. I will keep these women names off the record but my 1st good relationship was when I was very young, I would say maybe 7th grade. This young lady was amazing. She was beautiful, smart, great smile, outgoing and great personality. Now one of my biggest fears growing up would be that women would not want to talk to me because I was sick, but that wasn't the case with her, she wanted me for me. We just had a great relationship at that age. I know you're thinking that it's just puppy love but call it what you want. You can't help the way you feel about a person. We talked about any and everything. I treated her like the queen she was. Granted we were still young and I was still looking at other girls, in the end, I messed up the relationship. I really cared for her and if I would have stayed the course, there's no telling where we and our lives would be today. Even without me in her life now, she has married, has a child and a successful career. The worse relationship I can recall is a young lady I was dating in my twenty's. The relationship started off great, but don't they all until you finally see the true nature of an individual. I can't say that I was in love with her, but I had love for her. Things began turn rocky in the relationship when sabotages started to arise with female friends of mine at the time. Nothing was going on with me and my female friends, because we were friends before I got in that relationship. There's nothing wrong with having friends of the opposite sex. As things started to progress and get really out of control, I just had to call it off. Now, this was one relationship that I didn't mess up for it to end. After ending the relationship, strange things started to happen. You ever get that feeling somebody is following you. Well she was. She was stalking me. Everywhere I went, she would amazingly show up at that location. She wouldn't stop calling my phone so I had to change numbers. I had a real live stalker on my hand!!! These two relationships are just some relationship experiences that I went through while dating. I've had more good relationships than bad ones. I've had relationships that ended due to my illness. I've had women tell me they love me and when times get tough when I become sick, it's too much for them and they leave the relationship. In the clutch moments of my illness, I was able to find my fiancée, Ms. Solicia Coleman. She's means so much to me, in my life at this point. She has stood by me through thick and thin in dealing with my illness. She has seen me at my worse and my best and she is still here. She loves me for me and that means so much to have somebody love me for the person I am and can overlook something that I never had control of or asked for. God saw favor over me when he put her in my path.

My education as an adult started in August of 2001. I started attending the University of Arkansas at Little Rock where I started off majoring in Biology/Pre-Med. This is another great journey that I'm proud of. Being the 1st of my siblings to attend college was BIG for me and difficult at the same time. I've never been away on my own, so college would be my 1st test being away on my own and dealing with my diabetes. Growing up, I already knew what I wanted to do since I was a type 1 diabetic. I wanted to go to school and become a Pediatrician who worked with kids with type 1 diabetes. I felt I had a lot of knowledge about diabetes and could only gain more by my continuous studying of the illness. My college years were very challenging because I got sick from time to time and this would cause me to drop classes after missing so many which led me having to drop the entire semester. Being a Biology/Pre-Med major was tough. You have to always be studying. You don't really have time to have a social life or party. I saw this 1st hand from a good friend of mine I met while in college who was majoring to become a Pharmacist. As time went on, I would eventually have a child on the way and that was not for a Biology/Pre-Med major so I ended up changing my major to Business with an emphasis on Entrepreneurship and Small Business. I always had a business mindset along with some great ideas so this would be perfect for me. Through my trials and tribulations in college due to my illness, I was able to obtain my Business Management degree in May of 2011. It took me 10 years from the time I started college up until I received my degree, but I did it. I tell people all the time, it doesn't matter how long it takes you to get your degree, JUST GET IT!!! You can't control the bumps and obstacles in the path of your success, you just have to pick yourself up each time you get knocked down and continue to press forward.

Growing up in my family, church was all we knew, which I'm pretty sure that's most families in America. We would go to church several times a week. I accepted Christ in my life at an early age. I was baptized at the age of 5. I knew Jesus died on the cross for my sins. Still, today I believe in my Lord and Savior, Jesus Christ. I've been through a lot in my years of existence and I've come to realize that I don't have a religious relationship with my God, I have a spiritual relationship with Him. He has kept me for a long time with his grace, mercy and love. There aren't enough ways I can truly thank Him for all He has done for me, but I will continue to serve Him faithfully and stand on His word. Whatever His will is for me, I will be obedient and do it.

My feelings once I found out I had a lifelong disease had my emotions all over the place, but I can guarantee none of them were happy in nature. I'm a very nice, sweet and caring person, but people have said over the years that I have a mean demeanor about myself. I was very mad from day one when I got all the news about my new illness. I didn't quite know what was happening to me because I didn't know anything about diabetes, but things were starting to change for a 9 year old boy. I was mad when I got the news that sugar wasn't going to be my friend anymore, meaning that I can't eat sweets. Now how do you explain that to a kid? I was mad because I had to take 5 insulin shots daily and check my blood sugar 5 times a day, as well. I had moments in which I was sad because this was happening to me and not my other siblings. I learned that I was depressed. With so many mixed emotions, I ended up having to have counseling to cope with me being upset, mad, sad, depressed, and suicidal-the whole nine yards. I even questioned my faith. Why me? I didn't do anything to God to deserve this. I can say within those 20 years of my being sick, I stayed mad at the world for something they had no control over in my life.

My mother was hurt and confused because the doctor said I had a stomach virus when instead I was a diabetic. She was very scared and afraid that I wasn't going to make it. My sister Candi was mad and very upset. She wanted to know why we had to be the family that was different. She understands that we went through what the Lord needed us too, to make us stronger and as one, whole. My sister Danielle was hurt and sad because she was right there when everything was taking place and didn't quite know what was going on. She understand that no matter what I've been or went through she will always feel like that about her siblings because she will love us always. My sister Evonne thought it was the end of the world. She remembered our mother being very worried about me all the time because the doctor kept telling her that her baby had a stomach virus or something and for me to continue drinking sodas but come to find out the sodas was making me worse. My brother Le'Vorn was mad and upset, as well. Growing up he knew we were all we had as a family and now something like this was standing in the way of our bond. This was something new for him and my other siblings to have to take in on a whole different level of responsibility. My sister Sha's feelings were hurt!!! She kept wondering why and hoped that it would pass.

Yes, my sickness pulled my family closer together. Granted, we were already close but this event brought us even closer. We knew, as a family, if I was going to get through this, I needed them to understand my current world. My mother use to have my siblings get their blood sugar checked every now and then when I checked mine. This was her way of letting them know how my life would be for the rest of my life. We pulled closer together on the grounds that my family took a major interest on what to do if I ever got sick. My mother has been by my hospital bed every time but once or when I got older and told her not to come. With the knowledge base of my illness from my other siblings, they knew just as much about my illness to help me when needed.

The one thing that bothered me the most was the fact that I would have to take insulin shots for the rest of my life. This was my new life line since my pancreas stop producing insulin in my body. Now, I've never been afraid of needles but you only have limited stick sites and after a while they start to get really sore. I started out having to stick myself 5 times a day to try and keep my blood sugar level under control. Another thing that really bothered me once I started to receive important information on diabetes, was the fact that it was high on the cause of death among people with the disease. The life expectancy wasn't great for people with diabetes. A few years later after I was diagnosed, I lost my grandfather and my grandmother within a six month span because of diabetes. My diabetes was inherited from my grandparents on my father side of the family.

As for my career, I'm an Entrepreneur, as well as, a Network Marketer. I once worked in Corporate America, but when I became sick because of my diabetes, it caused my kidneys to fail and I lost a really good job. I had worked for the previous 9 years before this experience took place. I've always been a hard worker. Once I was cleared by my team of doctors to go back to work, no job really wanted to hire me. They said I had been out of work too long and that I should start at McDonald's or something of that sort. That was an insult in my eye especially when I have a BBA, Bachelors of Business Administration degree with an emphasis in Entrepreneur and Small Business. I've had some home-based businesses that I've worked before and this is how I make my living today. Having a job is a great place to start but not a great place to finish. After years of personal development, including books, audios, trainings, etc. I have come to realize that I can't go to work in Corporate America and make somebody else's dream rich when I have dreams of my own.

As of 2014, emotionally I'm blessed!!! I went through the test that God put before me and I passed. It was a tough and long journey but I endured and now I don't have to take those 5 shots a day. I don't have to worry about my sugar intake. I don't have to worry about watching what I eat, even though I still eat healthy. I've never been full of such joy and happiness in the past 22 years but I knew God would make a way out of no way. You must always stay ahead of your illness. Its chess, not checkers so you must be 3 moves ahead in advance. Follow all the rules of your doctors. Try not to stress over it as much. You have the disease now and there's nothing you can do about it but take care of yourself. Study this critical illness like the back of your hand as soon as you can. The more you know, the better prepared you will be when something arise. Lastly, try to live as much of a healthy life as you can. You're the deciding factor on how you control your illness or how you let your illness control you. Set personal goals for yourself when it comes down to controlling your blood sugar level and eating the proper foods.

Support!!! Support!!! Support!!! The one thing I use to tell my family is that, stop feeling sorry for me and saying that you understand what I'm going through. Until you can walk a day in my shoes, you will never know what a single day in my life is like. You must support that individual. You have to give him/her a lot of love as well. I think you should have talks about things other than the illness. It helps that individual know that life can still be normal. Don't show favoritism because it will only make the individual weak. That individual needs to be as strong as possible because everybody with Type 1 Diabetes is going to face some tough days and weakness that will take you out sooner than later. Help the individual to grow into his/her illness. This will put them in a comfortable position to accept all that is happening in their life. Also please help them to do right by this disease so they can prevent amputation. Once a diabetic is cut on or have an amputation, the cutting process never stops.

Since I have a passion for cooking, I hope to open my own restaurant one day. I think I will start with baby steps and open my own catering company first, then use my proceeds and networking to fund my restaurant. I will also continue to work my current Network Marketing companies to build a sustainable residual income. Building a residual income requires time, effort and patience but once it's done right, you have it locked in. Since this is my 1st book that I will be publishing, I would like to continue to write and hopefully become a Best Selling Author one day. All these endeavors will allow me to leave a legacy for my daughter and my future family. I'm engaged at the current moment and planning our wedding for 2015. All in all, I just want to continue to live a comfortable healthy life that God has blessed me to see, even though my ups and downs.

Little boys are known to jump, play rough and run as little boys often do, however; I didn't feel much like playing rough, running and jumping like normal little boys. I felt DIFFERENT. I could tell something strange was taking place in my body and I couldn't explain it. I knew something was not right, I was not normal. But why I not normal.......My journey of this abnormality am began in February of 1993, at the age of nine. I was only 9 years old at the time and something strange was taken place with my body. I had always been a very active kid. I had 4 sisters and a brother and being around my brother and sisters kept me having something to do for fun as a child. The latter part of the month of January showed me different. My daily activities started to slow down. I was more tired than ever. I didn't have the energy that an active 9 year would normally have. I became sick and this was a new experience for me because I normally didn't get sick. My mother took me to the doctor's office and my pediatrician diagnosed me with a stomach virus. Now 9 out of 10 times when a doctor diagnoses you with a stomach virus, they will put you on Sprites and meds to ease your stomach. I was prescribed a pink, thick, sweet medicine called penicillin. So for a few weeks I was on this medication along with Sprites. All this sugar, from the sweet medicine penicillin, is now going into my body. Even with me taking this medicine on a regular, because my mother made sure I did, I still wasn't getting any better. At this point my energy was at its lowest point. It was so bad that I needed help getting around the house. My mother kept saying that something else is wrong and she wants a second opinion because I should have been up playing by now. I didn't have the energy or want to do anything. I stayed thirsty and use the bathroom frequently. It wasn't until late one February night that I literally urinated on myself while I was sleeping. Now, I'm 9 years old at the time and never had a problem with my bladder so even I knew that shouldn't have happened. Something was SERIOUSLY wrong!!! I called for my mother and she came into the room and saw what had happened and said this is enough I'm taking you to the Emergency Room. My mother has always been a great woman, especially to her kids. After my accident, she would then clean me up and put me on some fresh clothes and take me to the Emergency Room. We made it to Helena Regional Medical Center where they saw the condition I was in and took me straight to the back. The normal procedures were being performed in the ER as if any other individual was in the back, blood pressure being taken, blood work being drawn up and a million and one questions being asked. My mother took care of the million and one questions while the physicians were doing the poking on me. I swear it felt like they took all the blood I had except what was need to still survive on until more was produced in my body. I can say that the next poke was a BIG one because it was my 1st but wouldn't be my last, I was getting an IV. As I stated before, this is truly my very 1st time being this sickly to the point where I ended up in the hospital. Hey I was like any other kid/boy who love to play outside, play rough etc., when I got hurt my mother would patch me up, kiss me and send me on my way, but this ER trip was new and scary. The scariest event would take place in the next couple of minutes. While my mother talked to the nurses and doctors on staff that night, my blood work would come back and show that my blood sugar was already 700+. Remember, a normal blood sugar range is considered 80-120 but this type of number sent the ER staff in total chaos. They started running around like chickens with their heads cut off literally; making phone calls, calling different departments in the hospital, getting the lab tech back down to retake my blood, getting my PCP (Primary Care Physician) up and out of his bed and on his way to the hospital and even writing up paperwork to have me transferred to a hospital that can handle a situation like this. After rechecking my blood sugar, the number was right because this time I was in the mid-800s. Numbers don't lie, so I was in a bad situation at that current moment. As I felt myself start to drift away, the staff at Helena Regional Medical Center was getting me ready to go to Arkansas Children's Hospital in Little Rock, Arkansas. From my hometown of Helena, Arkansas, Little Rock was about a 2 hour drive. The paperwork was finalized and the ambulance was ready to transport me to the best place the doctors thought would help me in my situation because they had done all they could do at Helena Regional Medical Center for me. I was loaded into the back of the ambulance while my mother sat in the front. Note that for this journey of being sickly, my mother has never left my side and I will forever love her for that. The blue and red lights started to flash and we were off and running. I was so out of it to the point where I just went along for the ride and got some sleep, or so I thought. I had actually gone into a coma on the way to Arkansas Children's Hospital. All my mother could do was cry and pray that I pull through. At this point, the ambulance was doing just above the speed limit to get me to Little Rock, Arkansas. I was being taken care of to the best of their ability in the back of the ambulance with what they had. We finally make it to Little Rock to Arkansas Children's Hospital and I'm immediately rushed to the back. If you thought the doctors and nursing staff were in a panic in my hometown, it was ten times worse here. I don't know how unique my case was, but, remember that my blood sugar was in the mid-800s as we departed Helena Regional Medical Center but now, I'm in a coma and my blood sugar has risen to 1400+ so I would classify my situation as being an unique one.

Chapter 1 (1993)

Diabetes is a lifelong disease and there is no cure. Type 1 diabetes can occur at any age. It is most often diagnosed in children, adolescents, or young adults. Insulin is a hormone produced in the pancreas by special cells, called beta cells. The pancreas is behind the stomach. Insulin is needed to move blood sugar (glucose) into cells. There, it is stored and later used for energy. In type 1 diabetes, beta cells produce little or no insulin. Without enough insulin, glucose builds up in the bloodstream instead of going into the cells. The body is unable to use this glucose for energy. This leads to the symptoms of type 1 diabetes. The exact cause of type 1 diabetes is unknown. Most likely it is an autoimmune disorder. This is a condition that occurs when the immune system mistakenly attacks and destroys healthy body tissue. With type 1 diabetes, an infection or another trigger causes the body to mistakenly attack the cells in the pancreas that make insulin. Type 1 diabetes can be passed down through families.

It was said that I could have inherited my diabetes from my grandmother on my father's side of my family. My mother had six children, 4 girls and 2 boys. I'm the oldest boy and 2nd oldest out of the six and I'm the only one that ended up with diabetes. I use to tell myself that I'm glad it was me ironically speaking because I'm strong enough to deal with it. My other siblings wouldn't have been able to make it through all I've been through. Not to say they are not strong in their own way but they wouldn't want to walk a day in my shoes. I'm the rock of my family and I would rather go through than to see them go through.

So how do you know if you have diabetes or what are the signs/symptoms of having diabetes? Understand that I have dealt with this disease for 20 years so I know it like the back of my hand!!! This quick educational piece will let you know if you or someone you know can have diabetes or if they need to go and get tested to see if they have diabetes or not. I would recommend to everybody in the world to go get tested/checked for diabetes at least once a year. Most cases of diabetes in the world are unknown. From there it's too late then there are more problems to deal with involving the disease like my situation was.

What would be my biggest challenge with being a 9 year old kid with Type 1 diabetes? Oh there will be quite a few. Close your eyes and think of the one food or type of food category that all kids love to have and eat. I'm pretty sure everybody thought of "candy". Outside of having a very strict diet, candy will become my downfall in this journey. I'm not going to lie to you and say that in my 20 years of being a diabetic that I didn't eat candy, wrong!!! I have sisters and a brother and we are all kids, having fun, doing kid stuff and eating sweets and candy. My mother did her best to not allow my siblings to eat certain things around me that I couldn't have. It was effective for the most part but I thought it was selfish. They didn't do anything to deserve that so why should they miss out on the things they loved. I told my mother to just let them be kids and enjoy life. I will have to deal the best way I can. This was only the beginning of what was one of many things that would make me stronger in my situation.

My first year with my new found illness would be a test of time for me, as well as, my mother. We have never been in a situation of such. I mean all kids get sick from your normal sickness; colds, fevers, stomach viruses etc. but nothing this big. For the next 20 years, I and my support team would have to focus on doing all that is required to keep me healthy and living.

After spending a few weeks in that coma when I was first diagnosed, I was monitored carefully before I was allowed to go home and continue my care there. Arkansas Children's Hospital in Little Rock will see and know me personally over the next few years. Being released to go home was a great feeling for a 9 year old kid. Hospitals are no fun. We make it home that morning after spending about a month and a half in the hospital and check my blood sugar. My blood sugar count was 505. I will never forget my 1st blood sugar check because I and my mother went into panic mode. We were taught in our classes that a normal blood sugar level should range between 80-120, so 505 was dangerously high. We would later realize that I was a special case because my blood sugar would always range high numbers. I would have to check my blood sugar 5 times a day. Checking your blood sugar level yourself and writing down the results tells you how well you are managing your diabetes. To check your blood sugar level, you use a device called a glucose meter. Usually, you prick your finger with a small needle called a lancet to get a tiny drop of blood. You place the blood on a test strip and put the strip into the meter. The meter gives you a reading that tells you the level of your blood sugar. You should always keep a record of your blood sugar for yourself and your doctor or nurse. The numbers will help if you have problems managing your diabetes. You and your doctor should set a target goal for your blood sugar level at different times during the day. You should also plan what to do when your blood sugar is too low or high. Low blood sugar is called hypoglycemia. Blood sugar levels below 70 mg/dL are too low and can harm you. Pricking your fingers 5 times a day, 7 days a week for 52 weeks in a year because your life depends on it isn't any fun and it leaves the tip of your fingers very sore and tender. That's 1820 pricks a year!!!

Because type 1 diabetes can start quickly and the symptoms can be severe, people who have just been diagnosed may need to stay in the hospital. If you have just been diagnosed with type 1 diabetes, you may need to have a check-up each week until you have reasonable control over your blood sugar. This is why I stayed in the hospital for a month and a half. Your healthcare provider will review the results of your home blood sugar monitoring and urine testing. Your provider will also look at your diary of meals, snacks, and insulin injections. It may take a few weeks to match the insulin doses to your meal and activity schedule. As the disease gets more stable, you will have fewer follow-up visits. Visiting your healthcare provider is very important so you can monitor any long-term problems from diabetes.

Type 1 Diabetes is more serious than Type 2 Diabetes. You are the most important person in managing your diabetes. Insulin is the KEY to Type 1 Diabetes!!! Insulin lowers blood sugar by allowing it to leave the bloodstream and enter cells. Everyone with type 1 diabetes must take insulin every day. Upon me leaving the hospital for the first time, I was put on 5 different insulin shots daily with 3 different types of insulin to use. I started off taking Humulin R (Regular), NPH (neutral protamine Hagedorn) and Humulin 70/30 (70% human insulin isophane) Suspension and (30% human insulin) Injection, [rDNA origin] types of insulin. Insulin must be injected under the skin using a syringe, insulin pen or pump. It cannot be taken by mouth because the acid in the stomach destroys insulin. Insulin types differ in how fast they start to work and how long they last. The health care provider will choose the best type of insulin for you and will tell you at what time of day to use it. Some types of insulin may be mixed together in an injection to get the best blood glucose control. Other types of insulin should never be mixed. You may need insulin shots from one to four times a day. Your healthcare provider or diabetes nurse educator will teach you how to give insulin injections. At first, a child's injections may be given by a parent or other adult. By age 14, most children can give their own injections. When I say I was a different case for being a diabetic, I never let anybody give me my shots. I will say in 20 years of having Type 1 Diabetes, I may have let somebody give me my shot twice, three times at the most. Even if I was too sickly to be doing it myself, I still did it.

People with diabetes need to know how to adjust the amount of insulin they are taking:

- When they exercise
- When they are sick
- When they will be eating more or less food and calories
- When they are traveling

This is a life and death situation on learning how to adjust your amount of insulin usage. I learned early on the consequences behind it. I love to cook, been cooking since I was 9 years old. This is my love/passion; what gets me away from everything. After being home from the hospital for a while I was frying some chicken and I hadn't eaten enough to cover my insulin intake and I passed out. My blood sugar had dropped tremendously and when I woke up, I was at the hospital. Low blood sugars will lead to a coma. You must always feed your insulin intake or episodes like this will take place.

Being a young kid you like to run and play with the other kids. Always know your blood sugar count before exercising. By testing your blood sugar level, people with type 1 diabetes learn which foods and activities raise or lower their sugar level most. This helps them adjust their insulin doses to specific meals or activities to prevent blood sugar from becoming too high or low. Regular exercise helps control the amount of sugar in the blood. It also helps burn extra calories and fat to reach a healthy weight.

This has been a challenging year by far but it's only the beginning. Unable to get my blood sugar levels under control would land me in the hospital every other month for 2 to 3 weeks out of that month. The more times I went into the hospital, I was learning something new about my new illness. Being a student of your situation can always put you in front of it at all times if you take it seriously. I was one to be taking it very seriously once I learned that diabetes is a top leading cause of death. What a journey so far for a now 10 year old but with God by my side, I can't lose.

Chapter 2 (2001)

Going off to college was a big deal for me. With my previous years with my Type 1 Diabetes, I wanted to go to school to become a Pediatrician and work with kids with Type 1 Diabetes. Developing juvenile diabetes at the age of 9 would allow for me to relate with my patients. I've never been away from home like this or away from my mother who has always been by my side to help take care of me. I knew that it was now time for me to grow up and do what is needed to survive outside of being under my mother's protection.

I'm in my senior year of high school and things are going according to plan. I'm still making great grades, building relationships with the right people for letters of recommendations and filling out college applications. Since I want to become a Pediatrician, I decided to apply to Xavier University of Louisiana in New Orleans. This university is one of the top medical institutions in which I could have received my teachings to become an outstanding Pediatrician. I decided to let my counselor do my financial aid application to the colleges I chose to hear get a response from. I'm feeling great about my next chapter in my life, while the end of my senior year is approaching fast. Graduation day is approaching faster than I think. I'm getting more excited than ever before because my passion to help others with the same condition that I have is going to become reality soon. A late Thursday evening while in class, I hear over the school intercom, "We need Quintion Little to report to the seniors' counselor's office". I'm thinking to myself that I can't be in trouble because I'm not a trouble-maker. I excuse myself from class and head to the counselor's office. I remind you that graduation is near and I'm expecting to hear from certain colleges for acceptance. I get to the counselor's office and I was then told that while he was filing out my financial aid package, he messed up and now I can't or won't be able to attend Xavier University of Louisiana to attend Medical School. It felt like my heart had dropped into my stomach. I was so hurt and crushed at the particular moment. This is my life's dream. This is what I had been working hard for. I had endured all the years of my Type 1 Diabetes to be able to help others cope and deal with this disease and now I won't be able to attend the school of my choice. This chain of events took away everything in me, but I still wouldn't allow myself to give up. One mistake or mishap on somebody's part doesn't dictate your life's plan. I basically put on my big boy pants and went back to the drawing board.

Graduation was approaching in two weeks. I have basically put the financial aid and counselor situation behind me because a new plan was in the making. As stated before, I've never just been away from my mother like this and going off to college in another state would be enormous for me but God is always working in my favor. In the last moments of figuring out where I would attend college, I was accepted to attend the University of Arkansas at Little Rock in Little Rock, Arkansas. I figured that I would do my basics there then transfer to Xavier University of Louisiana and cover my Pre-med courses and become the doctor I always wanted to be there.

Life in my eyes was still good. Every now and again I have an episode with my diabetes that has me bound to not accomplish anything. Being as sickly as I've been over the years can take a true toll on my body. There won't be a moment in life in which you will feel like giving up and throwing in the towel. Most people will never quite understand what you're going through or what you have been through because they can't truly walk a day in your shoes.

The time is here, GRADUATION 2001!!! This has been a great moment in my life. I've worked so very hard for this day. Many long nights of studying and no sleep has prepared me for this day. My high school experience was amazing. I built a lot of great friendships that will carry me into the near future. Even though I had times in which I missed weeks of school because of my Type 1 diabetes, I still was able to recover and graduate Top 10 in my class with Highest Honors. I've always felt that education is that key to the success of what I wanted out of life. You have to do something different to be able to get to the level of success and stability that you want; nothing will just fall in your lap. I've learned that the great ones had to go through the heartaches and pains to get to their land of milk and honey. I spent the week of my graduation thinking about all the ifs. What if I get sick and my mother isn't there to take care of me? What if I get so sick that I have to drop out of college and lose all hopes of my dream of becoming a Pediatrician? What if my focus needs to be on staying as healthy as I can and not go to college? What if? What if? What if? My mind had been racing for a week straight but my heart kept saying to live life and go after your dreams.

May 18, 2001 is one of many milestones in my life that I'm truly proud of, high school graduation. I truly have enjoyed my great friends, outstanding accomplishments, wonderful staff of teachers and just the journey but even with all of that, being sick can sometime outweigh all the good. I can truly remember my bad times from being sick over all the good memories I've had in high school. Over my 4 years, most knew about my illness but I still felt different. I had made a lot of friends and most knew the proper procedures to take if I were to get ill, however; that wasn't how I wanted them to always think of me. I was very popular in high school, Valentine's Court (9th grade), sophomore of the Year (10th grade), Class Vice President (11th grade) and even Prom King (12th grade) but I was still depressed most of the time and most didn't even noticed. I always gave off a nice smile and persona so that others wouldn't feel sorry for me. I consider myself strong but everybody has their weak and breaking points because at the end of the day, we are all human.

There's never a day without the chance of me getting sick. The morning of graduation I was very ill. I didn't think I would recover in time to attend my own graduation with my fellow classmates. I fought very hard to get myself back in shape to be able to walk across that stage and receive that high school diploma that I had worked so hard for and earned. With faith, determination and just the will to press on, I was up and ready for graduation. I had so many of my family and friends in town to see me graduate I couldn't let them down. Being the first one out of my mother's six children to graduate was a huge accomplishment. Nobody had time for sickness because the show must go on. I'm now fully dressed and headed to the high school to meet up with my classmates. We are all getting ready to embark on our very own journeys in life. High school graduation is a success and now I have the entire summer to lay out my next step of my future. Diabetes and being sick has been my entire life up this point, but I wanted better. I have seen the inside of a hospital hundreds of times up to this point and it will not be the last.

I've saved up some money for my first year in college from a summer program I enrolled in to help tutor children in learning the material for their proceeding grade. I wasn't able to have all the things I wanted coming up, so I had to get out there and make it happen for me. I was a teacher's aide in this brief summer program. I loved what I did because I got to interact with children and help them learn. I was able to make $1500 from the summer program which would help me get settled in college and my dormitory at school. I could use that money to buy some things for my room and get my books along with personal items. I didn't have the financial support from my family like most, but hey I managed with what I had and made the best of it without complaining. God is good and always on time. The summer program was only 4 weeks so after it was over, I spent the rest of my summer spending time with family and friends. I wanted to make sure that I showed my love to those who have been in my corner since day one helping me fight this hard and very difficult battle.

Just when you think you have everything in order for your departure, a roadblock or obstacle will arise and try to prevent you from achieving your goal. It's about a week before my official move in into my dormitory and I don't have a ride to Little Rock, Arkansas to attend school. I don't have a car otherwise I would have driven me and my belongings there myself. I'm getting stressed and very frustrated and that's not a good thing for me and anybody to be honest. Stress is a killer and with my health problems I don't need anything that could land me in the hospital before I get to start my college career. I started to do what I do best and that's come up with a good, no great plan. I reached out to my fellow graduated seniors and friends to see who else may be attending a college in Little Rock, Arkansas. After reaching out to a few contacts, BINGO, I found my solution. I was able to catch a ride to Little Rock, Arkansas with a friend of the family who was taking a fellow classmate of mine there attending another college. In the end, everything worked out and I was on my way to start a great college journey!!!

College life was different for me. This would challenge me more than ever. It's a 2 hour drive away from my mother and to make matters worse, she can't drive. If I were to get sick, how would she get to me? Remember, my mother has been there for me every step of the way since I've been sick. I was a little worried, but then realized that God has kept me thus far for a reason so I will get through this just like all other obstacles. It was time for me to become self-dependent, be a man!!!

The first semester of college was out of this world!!! I met so many new friends; made so many new networks and was just an all-around likeable guy. I did have an older cousin attending the same university so he should have kept me on the up and up, WRONG!!! I started off doing great in class. I was going regularly, doing homework and just being the student I grew up being. After a while, things started to change. I was hanging out with my older cousin and his friends and this was leading me to not go to class, having missed assignments and on the verge of failing. From time to time I got sick with my diabetes, but when you have been dealing with this for as long as I have, you know how to take care of the situation when it arise. I tried my best to stay out of hospitals, but with my condition and my blood sugar staying high all the time, I was there more than most.

I encountered some up and down events my first semester in college. One of my most feared moments came the morning of 9/11. As I awoke that morning in my regular routine, I didn't turn the television on. I just left my room and went downstairs to go outside before class to get some fresh air. As I approached the downstairs lobby, I noticed the majority of my new friends gathered in the lobby staring at the television. I would join them to find out all the disturbing news that was taken place. As I stood and watched with the others, it finally hit me, I have a close friend/classmate that moved to that area and was in harm's way by working closely to all the ongoing action. I didn't have a cell phone at that time but I needed a way to contact my friend. I had a number and was able to reach her and find out that she was ok. Thank God!!! Even with all I endure in life, I still have a heart for the people I care about.

As time went on and my first semester of college was drawing to an end, I had a major problem. I wasn't in a position financially to take care of most of my college expenses. After doing my calculations for the following semester, it came out that I could attend school with the aid I was receiving but I wouldn't be able to get my books for class. Books in college are very expensive. I called my mother and told her that after only one semester of college, my dream of becoming a Pediatrician was coming to an end because I didn't have the finances to get my books for next semester. This news crushed her. She has always known my passion for going to college to accomplish my dreams of becoming a doctor. Another defeat that the devil thought he had won but no no no, I and my mother put our heads together to come up with a plan. We were doing everything in our power to make my college life drive towards being on that right path. This is a lot for an 18 year old to take on along with being sick. Even though, I've found that the more pressure applied into my life, I fight harder for the best results. All our hard fought efforts were looking slimmer day by day. We weren't getting the proper results we needed to get the finances for books. Things were really starting to look as if I would not be able to attend college for a second semester. What to do? What to do?

December was fast approaching and the semester was coming to an end and I still didn't have a true game plan. One November morning would change my life dramatically!!!! We were out of school for the Thanksgiving break and I didn't go home but stayed on campus. One of the music industry's great R&B singers, Aaliyah had passed away on August 25, 2001. I was in the dormitory's computer lab on the BET's official website looking up information on Aaliyah's passing. While on the site, I noticed a link on the left of the page that said, "CONTEST". I loved the style of music Aaliyah had put out and was a big fan so after reading her information, I went back to the "CONTEST" tab and clicked on it. That tab took me to a contest that BET was having call "Jay-Z Get Your Book on Scholarship". The scholarship was for $50,000 giving away by famous rapper and business mogul Jay-Z, aka Shawn Carter. I read over the rules and decided to fill out the entry form. In my mind, this was a sign from God letting me know that not only was me and my mother working to get me money for books, He was and will always be working too!!! I would have never found this contest if I had never gone to the computer lab to read more about an artist that I love and adore. Sit back, buckle up and hold on tight because what I'm about to tell you next will blow your mind!!!

I actually skimmed through the contest rules and went on to fill out my information. Now I know you're thinking, college scholarship so the entry should include an essay, recommendations etc. but not here. The entry form consisted of my basic information; name, phone number, age, address, college and email and that's it, no essay or recommendations or anything of that nature. Can you say another blessing in the making??? So I filled the entry form out and walked away from it. I never went back to the contest to check on it or anything. I'm from Arkansas and I told myself that people from Arkansas don't win things like that. What's the catch of this $50,000 scholarship that I missed out on? Remember, I filled out the entry form once and walked away from it but the contest was set up for you to come back every day and re-enter your information every day until the contest ended to better your chances to win. WOW!!! I missed out on that opportunity. One entry so one shot at winning. I really needed financial help for books, as well as other things that were costly in college so Heavenly Father be with me...

Chapter 3 (2002)

It's now January 2002 and still no solution to my book problem but I didn't let that keep me out of school. I stayed in and said it will all work itself out. School hadn't started back for us yet which was a good thing because another episode had taken place with my Type 1 Diabetes. When I woke up that Tuesday morning, I knew it would be a bad day. I was having frequent urination, dry mouth, difficulty breathing and was super tired, but I had just slept for 8 hours or more. I have gotten to the point where I can tell if my blood sugar is high or low without even checking it and I have a 99.9998% accuracy rate in doing so. I knew my blood sugar was high but not as high as it was when I checked it. My blood sugar has always run high since I started this journey back in 1993. Since I only like to check my blood sugar when I'm feeling bad, it was time. Upon checking my blood sugar that day I got a reading of 600+. I was feeling super bad and when I get like this, the hospital is my only option. I had my cousin who was attending the same university with me take me to the ER and I knew they would keep me and they did. My blood work showed that all my blood gauges were all out of control. I even developed ketones in my urine. High levels of ketones can poison the body. When levels get too high, you can develop DKA. DKA may happen to anyone with diabetes, though it is rare in people with type 2. Treatment for DKA usually takes place in the hospital. Diabetic ketoacidosis is a problem that occurs in people with diabetes. It occurs when the body cannot use sugar (glucose) as a fuel source because there is no insulin or not enough insulin. Fat is used for fuel instead. Byproducts of fat breakdown, called ketones, build up in the body. Ketoacidosis is very bad and will require hospitalization every time. It's a serious condition that can lead to diabetic coma (passing out for a long time) or even death. Not the way I wanted to start off the New Year but this has been an uphill battle since day one. Since school wasn't starting back until another 2 weeks, I was going to be fine once classes started. I spent about a week and a half in the hospital getting everything back to normal. It's never easy spending time in the hospital and most of the time I was just thinking about what my life would be like if I was normal. You can always dream and wish for better days but understand that God makes no mistakes...

I get out the hospital just in time to start classes. As for my book situation, I had to do something that I didn't want to do. I ended up taking out a student loan to have extra money for books to be able to further my education. STUDENT LOANS!!! STUDENT LOANS!!! STUDENT LOANS!!! This will come back to haunt me in the long run. Now that everything is back on track, time to get my second semester of college going. The student loan that I took out with the help of my mother covered my books but left a little money after books were paid. I took some of that money and bought me a cordless phone for my room. This way I can keep in touch with my siblings and mother back home. Since this is the first time I've been away from them for this amount of time, I need a way to continue to communicate. As a family we kept in touch through writing letters, postcards and pictures. This was a comfort zone for me. Still to this day, I have a trunk full of letters and pictures from my college days sent from family and friends. I'm such a family oriented person and this was my escape from a hard week of class, a test or just being frustrated with being sick with my Type 1 Diabetes.

It is now 3 weeks into the new semester and as stated before, I got a cordless phone for my dorm room and it was ringing off the hook. Now who has my number other than family, newly made friends and well, a few women? When staying on campus in a dormitory, your phone line has a set number for each room. Because the cordless phone has caller I.D., I can see and know all numbers that were being dialed from the dormitory but this other number had my puzzled. So one day before heading out the door for class, the phone rings with the same number as before that I didn't know. I decide to answer it this time. This is how the conversation went:

Me: Hello.

Voice on other end: May I speak with Quintion Little.

Me: This is him. How may I help you?

Voice on the other end: This is one of the producers from BET.

Me: Man quit playing I got to go to class.

I would then hang up and head out the door for class so I wouldn't be late. My sister Danielle would call me from time to time just to see how I'm feeling. I get out of class and from sticking around in the student center, hanging out with friends, having lunch; I would then make it back to my room. I check the caller I.D. and my sister Danielle has called me a few times by now. I settle in and then proceed to call her back. We talk and I find out that the producers from BET have been trying to reach me and have called my mother's home to try and reach me. I did put that number on my submission form because at the time I didn't have a college number to give them.

My sister goes on to tell me that they will be calling me back in the next couple of days to try to reach me again. I tell my sister I love her and will call her and let her know what they say. Understand that I'm still at a loss for what is going on and why BET is calling me. Remember I filled out the entry form once and walked away from it thinking nobody in Arkansas will win anything of this magnitude.

Approximately 3 days after speaking with my sister on this situation, BET calls back and this time I'm ready!!! I'm in my room to take this important call and I was more than amazed at the news I got. After our formal introduction yet again, our conversation went like this:

James (Producer): Mr. Little I'm calling to inform you that you were the winner of the Jay-Z Get Your Book on Scholarship.

Me: Thank you so much. What did I win?

James (Producer): A cash scholarship from rapper Jay-Z. Do you remember the amount of the scholarship?

Me: Puzzled...um $20,000.

James (Producer): No Mr. Little, you have won $50,000 and a trip to be on BET's 106&Park in New York.

Me: Drops the phone and runs out the room screaming and yelling at the top of my lungs!!!

When I tell you that I was so excited, nervous, happy, feeling faint and any other emotion you want to put in there all at once. I had ran up and down my hallway to the point that I forgot that Mr. James was still on the phone. I pulled myself together and went back to my room to finish our conversation. After talking with the producer for another 30 minutes or so, I got all the details for the upcoming events that would take place with me winning this contest. I was super excited about the fact that the show was going to send a producer and camera crew to the university to film me for entire day to use as a segment for the show when I go to 106&Park. Oh yeah, I was going to New York as well!!! As we got ready to end the call, Mr. James said something that sent chills through my body. He told me that millions had entered that contest and there was an option to go back every day to enter again to better the odds of a person winning and I only entered once and won. Can you say blessed? What an on time God!!! He knew what I needed and when I needed it.

I called my sister to tell her the good news. She was so happy for me. I was giving a second ticket to bring somebody to New York with me and I told her she could have the other ticket since she was taking the calls from the show and because she kept me informed. Without her, I could have missed out on my blessing. I told my mother and the rest of my siblings my great news. At this moment, it still hasn't sunk in...$50,000!!!

It's a lovely spring day in March. The weather in Little Rock, Arkansas is a crisp 78 degrees. The sun is shining bright. I awake from my slumber and get ready to start my day. First class of the day starts at 8:00 a.m. sharp. I'm dress, books in backpack and ready to start this day. I open my door to head downstairs and there is a camera crew from BET waiting for me and started filming as soon as they seen me. This is so exciting. This is a live taping. No cuts, no retakes, no do overs, just taping me as I go about my day as if they wasn't even there. All of this was approved by the Dean of the university. It's a great honor to have something like this represented at my alma mater, the University of Arkansas at Little Rock. Today was one of my days in which I only had two classes to attend. Me and the camera crew went to class then ended up in the Student Center for lunch. Most of my friends were in there just hanging out and eating their lunch before their next class so they were caught on camera as well. The producer and camera crew showed a lot of love to everybody on campus that day. Lunch is coming to an end for most and the producer wanted to get me in a piece in front of the main signage of the university. The main goal here was to get some pictures and a brief dialogue of me talking to use in the segment when it airs. After finishing up, we went back to the dormitory and did a shot in the computer lab where I signed up for the contest. They had me to do a reenactment of me logging on, going to the BET site and looking around. They also did interviews with some of the residents in the computer lab at that time. I was enjoying this life time experience that I was going through. Most of the day is gone and we do things at the dormitory as a family and tonight a lot of us and the RAs (Resident Assistance) decided to go bowling. Even though the filming was over, the producer decided to come out to the bowling alley with us and get some more footage to use. We have a ball the rest of the night at the bowling alley. The producer and his camera crew are only in town for a day and have a flight to catch the following day. After we get back to the dormitory from bowling, I talk with the producer briefly before they head to their hotel. I sign all my paperwork and ask a few questions on how all this will take place. The producer was very helpful.

I say my goodbye for now and they head to their hotel to rest for the remainder of the night.

I get the call from the producers of BET that it's time to come to New York and do the show on 106&Park. They inform me that I would be there for 1 day and 2 nights, just long enough to get the show done and get me back to school to finish out the semester. I was also informed that I would have to fly. Now I've never flown and there's nothing wrong with flying. I've always wanted to fly but my 1st flight has to be to New York, right after 9/11. Umm, I don't think so!!! This is in no way how to have your very 1st flight....I told the producers that I would drive to New York to do the show. They said that couldn't be done and if I don't fly I don't get my $50,000. I said, "What time do the plane leave"? Originally I had told my sister Danielle she could get the other ticket to go to New York with me since she helped me in the process but unfortunately she was only 17 at the time and you had to be 18 or older to go. I asked my mom and she didn't want to attend. I asked my oldest sister Candi did she want to attend because she is 3 years older than me and she qualified to go but she had a prior engagement already. This was getting very frustrating and stress isn't something I needed with my condition. All of my other siblings were under me so that was out of the picture. I wanted somebody to experience this with me. I had one last option in my bag and prayed that it would work. I asked my cousin that was attending the university with me did he want to go. Because we were going in the first week of May, he couldn't attend because he was taking finals. I would also be taking finals but because of this I got an excuse from the Dean and my teachers. Plan A-Y has failed for finding someone to go to New York with me. There was still time for me to find someone and I thought I had exhausted all my options so I prayed about it and I got an answer. I had become good friends with the Resident Hall Director and I gave him the opportunity to go to New York with me. Thank God my prayers have been answered!!! I think I'm set and ready to go experience this grand opportunity and then I get another call from BET. My original trip was for 2 days, 1 night but some things came up on their end and I was given a 4 days, 3 night's trip to New York. Can you say ECSTATIC? This just keeps getting better and better.

The day has arrived for me and my friend to take flight. We were booked an early flight so we had to be at the airport by 5:30 a.m. for check-in. Now the flight wasn't expected to take-off until 7:00 a.m. but with the events of 9/11 in New York, a few months back, security has really tighten up. After check-in, we are just waiting so I decide to check my blood sugar to make sure everything is good because this is my very 1st flight and I'm already super nervous and don't need to be getting sick. Everything is good as far as my health; I'm feeling fine besides the fact that I'm nervous.

Our flight is on the runway and it's time for us to board the plane. It is such an early flight that once we get on the plane, there was only a handful of people on the flight that I was able to get a window seat and row all to myself. The flight attendant said it would be fine that I sit anywhere I chose because we have a layover in Atlanta. The Captain comes over the loudspeaker and let us know that we're about to take off. First flight experience and I'm ready. The plane turns and lines up with the runway. The plane starts to move and gather speed. Once the Captain has obtained the proper amount of speed, he pulls back on the stick and the plane lifts up into the air. I didn't care too much for the takeoff. The thrust of the speed and the sudden lift off snapped my body backwards to my seat. Once we got in the air and was level, the Captain took the plane up over the clouds. Oh what a site to see. It was as if there was a whole other world up there. It was such beautiful scenery. The flight from Little Rock, AR to Atlanta, GA was a short one. Now here is where the problem comes in with a 1st time flyer. As we get ready to approach Atlanta, it is storming a little and we are getting some turbulence. The plane is shaking and doing all type of stuff that I'm not use to. My only thoughts at this moment is, God see us through this. We make it through the turbulence and land at the airport in Atlanta before we have to switch planes for our final destination which is New York. Heavenly father I've made it through my 1st flight and I'm still here, THANK YOU!!!

The layover in Atlanta was about 2 hours. We found time to do things around the airport. My friend also had family and friends in Atlanta and some of his family came to the airport to hang out with us until our next flight got prepared to take off. We are now on our 2nd flight and destination is New York. This flight was jammed packed so I couldn't have an entire row to myself; I had to sit in my assigned seat. This flight would take a little longer than the first flight so I decided to take a brief nap. I still got a window seat on this flight as well. As we got ready to enter the state of New York, my friend woke me up so I can see some amazing sites of the city. As we came in, I saw the Statue of Liberty.

We are now at JFK Airport in New York, NY!!! We get our luggage and see a sign with my name on it. The producers of BET have sent a limo to come and pick us up and take us to our hotel. What a way to welcome somebody to the city, a limousine. Can't get any better than that. We are taken to our hotel which is in the heart of Times Square. Everything would be in walking distance for us. A 5-star rated hotel, everything is paid for, I'm ready to get this 4 days and 3 nights going. Never really been on a trip like this and most people would love to come to New York and don't get that opportunity to do so and I'M HERE...

We spend the first couple of hours settling in our hotel room and see what we can get into since the taping of the show isn't until the following evening. Being first time New Yorkers, we just decided to walk the streets and sight see. We met a lot of friendly people in the city. We went to some great tourist spots and just basically took it all in. As the night fell, we started to head back to our room to prepare for the show but more importantly, sleep. A few blocks from the hotel was a guy on the street doing drawings of people. I thought what a great gift to give my mother for Mother's Day coming up in a week or two. The guy did a self-portrait of me with only a pencil and it came out great. This is just some of the things that can be done in the city of New York, amazing talent. We make it to our room and turn in for the night or rather the morning because it was after 3:00 a.m. when we made it in from all the fun we had.

It's a brand new day and it's Showtime!!! We get ourselves up and get dressed for the BIG day. As we make it downstairs in the lobby to be picked up and taken to 106&Park, another limousine is outside waiting for us. We have been riding in a limousine everywhere we have been except when we went out in Times Square on our own. The limo driver takes us to the 106&Park studio and as we were pulling up, there was a line wrapped around the block waiting to get in the studio. We enter the studio and then introduced to the other producers as well as the host of 106&Park, A.J. and Free. I have my own backstage dressing room while I wait to be taking to the set of 106&Park. I sign my consent form and the show is ready to begin. I was kept behind the set until it was my time to appear. I was on the show in which rapper Cam'ron debuted his song, "Oh Boy". After interviewing Cam'ron, the show went to commercial break and then they brought me to the front to sit in the audience. I was sitting there and you could tell that I was super nervous. The host Free came and sat with me in the audience and talked to me for a while before the show came back on air. She told me to calm down and just be you when the cameras come back on. Easy for you to say when you have millions on top of millions of people watching this show. I grabbed my composure and was ready when the show came back from their commercial break. As I sat in the audience, they introduced the world to who I was and then showed my clip from the university when I was followed around for a day. After that, Jay-Z came through the curtains, I was brought up on stage and Jay-Z presented me my check with my $50,000 check. Of course it wasn't a real check but I got a big check like they give away when people win the lottery. You would have thought I had won the lottery after that moment. With the schedule being so tight, I was able to take pictures with A.J., Free, Cam'ron, Dame Dash and Jay-Z before we had to leave and head back to my hotel room. An exciting couple of hours that I will cherish for the rest of my life!!!

The last couple days left in New York was just as exciting as the first couple of days. On our last day there, we got the chance to ride to subway and go to his family house and eat some southern comfort food. I was surely missing this. If I had a stove and groceries in my hotel room, I would have done it myself. After spending a couple of hours there, we said our good byes and took the subway back to Times Square. The location the subway dropped us off at was only a couple blocks from our hotel. As we walked back to the hotel, NBC was having a 75th Anniversary parade. We were able to see actors and actresses from shows like Cheers, The Cosby Show, The Golden Girls and Friends just to name a few along with New York's finest, the police and fire department. What a way to end a trip!!! We check out the next day and head back to JFK Airport heading home.

The spring semester is coming to an end and since I'm a Biology/Pre-Med major, I want to attend summer school to knock some classes off my list. Summer classes require your finances up front to attend. If you don't have the money to attend, the university will allow you to apply for student loans. I don't want to have to apply for student loans again especially since I've won $50,000. Now I still haven't gotten my physical check for $50,000 but it's for me to pay for school so I called the producers to see if they could do something. Now originally they were supposed to send the check to the university and let the school disperse the money out every semester for my expenses but since I needed it sooner than later, they sent me a $50,000 check and told me to open a bank account and pay for my schooling that way. Wait a minute; I'm only 19 years old when all this is taking place. I've never had this amount of money in my possession at one time; Cha-Ching!!!

I opened up a checking account and deposited that $50,000 in it. When I went to the bank to make the deposit, the tellers were looking at me strange but hey the check was real and it was time for me to have some fun. Now I know what you're thinking, that money is supposed to be used for schooling. Trust me it will be along with other things...To sum up the remainder of my 2002 year, I bought me a brand new car of the lot cash, did some other things for my mom and siblings, help some friends out and just partied, partied, partied with some of that $50,000. I had partied so hard that I was missing class, my grades had dropped and it had got to the point where the university made me sit out a semester of school to get myself together. Now I never did anything that got me in trouble, just too much partying and missing class that landed me in this position. Making good grades was never the problem, I was just a young 19 year old enjoying a new lifestyle that I had no true leadership and guidance with. You live and you learn right???

Chapter 4 (2003)

When I was forced to sit out of school a semester for all that partying I was doing and allowing my GPA to fall, I left with a nice size amount of that $50,000. This allowed for me and my cousin to get an apartment together. Going back to my hometown wasn't an option for me, so we got an apartment in Little Rock. I thought that being off campus for a semester would allow for me to regain my focus but I was totally wrong.

My life took a full turn, from one end to another and I started indulging in things that people would never think I would do. I still had access to a nice piece of that $50,000 left and the partying didn't stop just because I was off campus. Actually the partying increased. See I didn't need to get a job to help out with the bills, I had the money and I just gave my half when it was time. ***This portion of my autobiography is all about the things I did, nobody else.

I was always known as the good boy coming up. I made the grades throughout high school. I wasn't a troublemaker. I grew up in the church. I was a gentleman and very respectful. I was the guy that a young lady could bring home to meet her mother. I don't want to say that the events leading up to this point was in no shape a lifestyle that I thought I would ever have. We all have done things in our past or life that we wish we could take back. How I was spending my $50,000 wasn't one of them but becoming a street pharmacist or drug dealer is. I indulged in a world that would have gotten most either killed or in jail. I wasn't into the hard stuff but just selling marijuana and I did pretty well. Never being in this type of business I had to learn the hard way of how to conduct this properly without getting myself robbed, killed or put in jail. I can tell you this, the money behind this industry is GREAT but the risks are TERRIBLE. I had over $25 to $30 grand left from my winnings so why would I need to do this. To this day I don't have the answer to that question. I didn't live this lifestyle for long but long enough to make some good money from it. I even decided to get a job in the process. Now I have my $50,000 winnings, money from my dealings and now a job; money on top of money on top of money. It was only a part-time job just to show steady income coming in. Understand that we all make mistakes in life and nobody is perfect. So what person do you know that is selling a product or service and doesn't use it? Not many. Yes, I use to smoke marijuana too!!! This is a bad thing for a person with my health conditions.

Taking care of your feet is a major thing when taking care of your diabetes. People with diabetes are more likely than those without diabetes to have foot problems. Diabetes damages the nerves. This can make you less able to feel pressure on the foot. You may not notice a foot injury until you get a severe infection. Diabetes can also damage blood vessels. Small sores or breaks in the skin may become deeper skin sores (ulcers). The affected limb may need to be amputated if these skin ulcers do not heal or become larger, deeper, or infected. Now to prevent such things as amputation or problems with your feet, you shouldn't smoke. In my 20 years of Type 1 Diabetes, I did everything within my power to stay away from having any amputations done. See once they start cutting on you, they will forever cut you. Since it takes a diabetic's body longer to heal than a normal person, most cuts, sores, amputations take longer to heal and in doing so may set up an infection. This will land you

right back in the place you don't want to be, the hospital. This is my story and I must let the people know the real and truthful me. Smoking marijuana for me was my scape goat to ease my mind from all the problems I faced daily with my health. It was my oasis or getaway from EVERYTHIING!!!

I had this one episode with smoking marijuana that would land me in the ER then be admitted in the hospital. I was going through the motions of being ill and depressed about life. I awoke one morning smoking with some friends and since it was an off day from work, I would continue to smoke all day and night. Once my cousin got home from work, he found me in my room barely able to move. I had to be picked up and carried to the emergency room. I was diagnosed with a serve case of dehydration. I ended up staying in the hospital for about 2 weeks to get plenty of fluids and my electrolytes back to normal. Life lesson learned!!!

Dealing drugs would end for me when I was told by the young lady I was dating at the time that she was pregnant. This is a life-changing event for me. I will never forget the call. I was so excited and nervous about the news. I cried and felt like vomiting all at the same time. See I was super excited because I knew I was going to be a great father to my future son or daughter. Now I was nervous because hey I was about to be a father and this is my 1st child. Now I have nieces and nephews that I have helped raise and take care of but not my own so this is BIG in my world. On the journey of becoming a dad will have you thinking about a lot. I had to realize that it isn't about me anymore so I can't continue to do the things that I'm currently doing. With that being said, I left dealing drugs alone and started my focus on my future child. There was no more going to the mall and spending money like crazy. No more going out to clubs and hanging out with my friends. No more spending unnecessary money anymore. No more!!! No more!!! No more!!! It was time for me to put my grown man pants on and be a true man and I was so ready for the challenge. See when most meet me; they say that I'm way more mature than my age.

Now what's left from that $50,000 isn't going to help raise this child so to the drawing board I went. Now I already had a part-time job that was put in place due to me selling drugs but now it was time to step the game up a notch. I went out day in and day out looking for something full time. I just wanted to have money saved and ready to start my relationship off with my son or daughter the right way. I kept working at my current part-time and went to ask to go full-time which I was granted that position. Step 1 is complete but for me that isn't enough. Even though I went full-time, it wasn't great on the pay so back to the drawing board I went. One of my managers at my current job was a teacher at another program with kids with disabilities. At this job they would have the children lunches delivered by a family owned catering company. One day she notices that the normal guy didn't deliver the order to the program, but the actual manager did. Come to find out that the previous guy had quit and the manager had to pick up the slack because he didn't have anybody else to do it. After talking with the manager and finding out he needed help, she got all the information and gave it to me. I always say God put certain people in your life for a reason. I took the information and went to the job site on a Wednesday and spoke with the manager. I got hired on the spot and started the next day. Since the job only worked Monday through Friday, I worked for two days and got paid that Monday because that was their payday. I thank my other boss for getting me that information and helping me to get a second job. Now I kept both jobs for a while to make and save as much money as I possibly could.

I started J&F Food Service as a delivery driver in October of 2003. My daughter is expected to be born the first week of December so I kept working both jobs. I was working one in the morning and one in the evening. This worked out for me, 5am to 1pm and 4pm to 10pm. I was tired but my focus was on my little girl arriving soon. J&F Food Service was owned by the Millers and they took real good care of me. They treated me like a son, as if they had me. I felt right at home even though we were of a different race. I will forever be grateful for what the Millers have done for me in my life within my time with them. They hold a special place in my heart.

After going to the last doctor's appointment for my daughter, we were told that if she doesn't come as scheduled they would have to induce the labor and take her. I started preparing myself for this moment. I have gotten time off from work to be able to go home and be there for the delivery of my daughter which at this point we decided to name her Diamond. December is here and it's game time. We go into the hospital on December 7, 2003 and 2 days later, on December 9, 2003 Diamond Lasha Nicole Little was born!!! Through everything I've been through with my diabetes up until this point, she is the BEST thing that has happened to me in my life!!! With me living in one city and my daughter's mother living in my hometown, I stayed in town with my daughter for the next 2 weeks. I never thought it was a true thing when people would say love at first sight but that's how I felt when I first saw and held my daughter. I loved her in her mother's womb but when she arrived, it was true love at 1st sight. I have truly loved my Diamond princess since day one and have continued to do so. She's my everything, daddy's little princess...

Chapter 5 (2004)

Starting the New Year off in 2004, life is good. I just had my baby girl born in December, still working two jobs, a great relationship and not too many problems with my Type 1 diabetes. With 2 jobs and my daughter living in my hometown, I try to make it home every weekend that I'm off from my evening job because my morning job is only Monday through Friday. If I can't make it every weekend, I'm going home every other weekend. I grew up without my father in my life so I know how important it is to be in my child's life. I told myself that I would be the BEST dad to my daughter that I can and I am living up to it. Being around her in the beginning stages of her life is so critical. You get to leave an imprint on her while she gets familiar with who you are. I can't say this enough but I just love my baby girl, Diamond Little!!!

Sometimes life can be going to good and then you hit a bump in the road. Just as quickly as your life and be going up up, you can take a massive blow and get knocked down down....

So one nice sunny day I get off work and run a few errands before I head home. As I leave out and head home on a normal route, you would think things will go as planned. As I make a turn on the street that my apartment is on, I'm literally 2 blocks from my apartment then it happens. I'm getting ready to pass a car so I go around the car on its left side and then out of nowhere, the car decides to make a left turn. BOOM I'm hit!!! I would then swerve to miss from making this wreck worse than what it ended up being. I run my right front side of my car on the curb and completely tear my front axle and tire rods while in the process breaking my 18' rims. Once the accident is all over, I had a front right rim and tire lying on the ground. At first I wanted to just drive it home and then get it towed but after assessing the damage, it wasn't possible. Proper protocol is taken and the police arrive and get statements and I'm cited with the bigger ticket and told that it was my fault. Now being young and dumb and riding dirty (no insurance) I ended up getting sued by the other driver. From this day forward all the madness begins....

With bills, a new born daughter and no car but two jobs, I just didn't have the money to do anything let alone get my car fixed. Since I didn't have any insurance, I would have to pay for my own damages as well as the settlement with the other driver. After accessing my damage to my car, I would have to come up with $2900 to get it fixed. Where would I get that type of money??? Now I know you're thinking, where is the remaining of the $50,000 you had won? Well let's do a quick recap of it. I won it in 2002, got an apartment in 2003 and now it's early 2004, I have a daughter to help take care of and did I mention I'm still very young in age. So again in the end I didn't have it. I don't regret anything I did with the $50,000 because I help my family and friends as well as strangers because that's the kind of heart I have. Now I will say that if I knew back then what I know now, I would have invested a portion of that money to keep it growing. Now I'm in thinking mode, what can I do???

I have a lot on my plate for just little ole me but hey I'm in a grown man's world so I have to find the solution. Now I'm good with math/numbers so I come up with a plan to save money while taking care of my daughter and paying bills because our lease isn't up just yet. This is harder than I planned because I'm working two jobs and trying to get to both of them on a daily basis because I need them but my cousins came through for me. This only worked for so long because now the lease on the apartment that I and my cousin got was up. This has put more stress on me.

With everything taking away from my finances, I didn't have the money to get my own place or get another place with a roommate and be responsible to handle my part. I didn't want to go back to my hometown of Helena, Arkansas. I left there to better myself and I wasn't turning back. Now I love my hometown and I know that you can always go home is the saying but just wasn't ready to do that.

After the official move out of the apartment, my cousin went his way and I ended up homeless. See most people didn't know that. Now homeless can be defined in so many ways. I wasn't laying on the streets at night homeless but I was staying from house to house homeless. I had no car, I was saving a much as I can but it was little and I really couldn't help those that were helping me so I move around from house to house. See I like to be a helping if you're helping me. This was very nerve wrecking. I couldn't put too much stress on myself because stress and diabetes would have my blood sugar readings out of control. It took years to get some type of control of my blood sugar readings but I still had a very high blood sugar when checked.

Running out of options; on my last leg, I felt as if it was time to go home. My cell phone is the only true bill I can keep on while saving because my health condition is bad so if something happens I need to make a call. As I still think hard on whether

I should move back to Helena, I give my oldest sister Candi a call. At this point and time she's still living in Helena, Arkansas. We talked for hours that day and it felt good to get a lot of things off my chest. See I'm the first out of my mother's six children to go to college and everybody wanted me to make something great of myself. She told me to let her make some calls and see what she could do about my living arrangements. We speak again a few days later and she has set up a living arrangement with one of her aunts on her father's side of her family. Now this was a permanent place for me to live until I could get my car fixed and get me a place to live but see I'm stubborn and didn't want to take the deal because I can't help out. She said that her aunt said not to worry about it, just come on with whatever I had because she considers me family. Whew… (Wipes forehead). God is good.

Things are starting to look up for me now. I have a place to live comfortably at the current moment and I still have one of the two jobs that I once had. Since I didn't have proper transportation to and from work, I couldn't work both jobs at the time. Remember that great family named the Millers that treat me like I was a son to them; they would make ways and arrangements to come pick me up for work and drop me off. I am a good hard worker so they did everything they could do to help me keep my job and save money in my current situation. You couldn't possibly understand the love I have for this family and we are of two different races!!! This is something I have never experienced but I have embraced it and I love it.

I have a secure roof over my head so now my focus is my car. $2900 is a lot to come up with but I have an older cousin name James that would have me on this journey to get my car fixed and back on the road. At this time, James had moved to Texas so he wasn't local but you would have thought he was. I was saving as much as I could while still doing what was right and giving at the location I was staying at. My mother raised me right and this was just the right thing to do. As time moves along, this plan is starting to work out for me.

Doing this journey I lost my way with Christ. I've only been in Little Rock, Arkansas for 3 years now and I didn't have a church home. When I stayed at the dormitory on campus, some of the college students and I would go to a local church down the street but I never made it my church home. There was a void inside of me, I was missing something...I was born and raised in the church by my mother, grandmothers and family members back home. I confessed my love to Christ and was baptized in 1988 so I know where I need to be and what I needed to be doing during my situation. A guy at my job, at J&F Food Service was talking about church one day and I started listening to his conversation. He plays the keyboard for his church and they had a gospel fest coming up and he asked me did I want to join him and his family. Since I didn't have a solid church home, I said yes I would love to go. What a great time I had at the gospel fest!!! I enjoyed that event so much that I started attending his church on Sundays. What I loved about his church was the fact that it was a family orientated church, small like from back home not a mega church, and filled with good people. I would later re accept Christ in my life and become a member of New Rock Hill Baptist Church under the leadership of Pastor Victor Nelson.

As of today, I'm still a member of New Rock Hill Baptist Church. Over the years I've gotten so much love and support from the church family with me dealing with my illness. Again I have found another close knitted family that loves me for me and have taken me under their wing. I'm just so drawn to people. I keep a smile on my face while I'm hurting inside but my goodness and personality can win anybody over. I became very active in my new church home and was at church every Sunday; even on Sundays when I was too sick to go but God gave me the strength to make it to his house of worship. Church on Sundays was my release and how I would start my week off on a good note. The second great family I owe so much too, the Nelson family...

Chapter 6 (2007)

At this point in my life I felt like nothing was going right. Being sick isn't fun at all and majority of the time it will stop you from accomplishing things. I start to look at things around me and saw that not only my stress of the world but the stress others were putting on me. Not that I'm one to worry about people in that sense, but I do have a kind heart that I get from my mother, therefore; I will worry and stress for others. I know that stress isn't my best friend with my health condition but I was having some family problems as well as something different was taking place with my body. I have been dealing with my Type 1 diabetes for quite some time now so I can tell you what's going on with my body before the doctor comes back and gives me the diagnosis. This was different; I've never felt this type of sickness before so that's when I knew something was wrong. When dealing with my diabetes and something new comes up that I have no knowledge of, I do what's best for me and go see a doctor.

I make an appointment and go see a doctor to find out what is going on. I get there and they do a full physical on me so they can cover all areas. I was asked a series of questions while there to see if something could be of interest to the physician for him to test for as well. The only thing I could tell him that was different for me was the fact that my vision was getting more blurry than before. All tests are done and I would now get a call in a week or so to give me my results.

So a week and a half rolls by and I receive a call from the doctor's office. I was asked what is the earliest I could come in so he could go over my test results. Since I'm in college at the moment I would be very flexible because I made my own schedule for attending class. I replied and told them I would be in that Friday since I have no classes on that day. Trust me when I tell you that I'm super nervous about going in about my results. Normally when your doctor's nurse call you back and nothing is wrong they tell you over the phone but this wasn't the case so I knew it could be bad. I really don't need any more bad news of health right now because dealing with diabetes is a large pill to swallow within itself. No matter the outcome of my health, I always call my rock, my mother, and let her know what's going on with me.

Friday is here and my appointment is scheduled for 1:00 pm. I check-in and wait to be seen by the doctor. My doctor comes in and gets right to the point. He says, Mr. Little, you have hypertension or high blood pressure.

I reply, how?

The doctor goes into various ways of me getting high blood pressure; stress, smoking, salty foods and other ways of having hypertension. Once he laid those options down to me, I was guilty as charged. I love to cook, so having my food seasoned right is my way of making food that sings to the taste buds of a person's mouth, guilty. We already know that I've been smoking marijuana since high school, guilty yet again. Now my stress is the biggest factor I thought about once the doctor said it. Living with Type 1 diabetes is stressful within itself. I go to bed and have nightmares about if I will wake up the next day because I might go into a coma while sleeping. Will I have to have a limb amputated? Will I lose my sight or go on dialysis? So many things go through my mind day in and day out. I also stress about my family too. Nothing or nobody is perfect in this world and from time to time as a family, we have fallouts. That's common but because we are family, things always blow over and we are right back to being the tight knit family that we were. All families have problems here and there. During this time in my life we were having family problems that stressed me a lot because at the end of the day, family is all we got. I don't like to see my family having problems with one another so this caused me to stress. It was more pressure on me with our family problems because I'm the rock, the glue that holds this family together. Even in the midst of all I go through myself, if I can't get things back right, then I have failed myself and my family and that's very stressful.

So after talking with my physician and getting some medications to help with my hypertension, I was ready to control yet another obstacle in my life that I wouldn't let win. That same night before bed, I think I prayed the hardest I've ever prayed before. I prayed for strength and guidance to get through this tough time because I was scared. God has kept me this far so I know this is just another test.

I'm not going to say that I jumped right into this and was doing everything that the doctor told me to do because that would be a lie. It was hard starting out because I had to retrain myself on how to do things. My biggest challenge would be my cooking habits. At the point in my life I've been cooking for 14 years now. I was told that instead of salt and certain seasonings to use a salt substitute like Mrs. Dash. I tried it out for a while but have you tasted that stuff??? I can't do it. I kept smoking because remember that was my oasis away from all my problems at times. This was harder than I thought.

I would start to get sick more often now because I didn't know if my blood sugar or my pressure was up, but both being up at the same time landed me in the ER plenty of times for symptoms of dehydration. Eventually, I had to scale back on some of the things that I was doing and do them in moderation.

Even in doing things in moderation I was still having problems from time to time. I had to continue to have visits to the physician's office to have him adjust my blood pressure medications. This was sort of a trial error for me to find out what was or wasn't working. Now with me having no insurance, it was hard for me to continue seeing a doctor let alone getting the blood pressure medications. Now you're probably thinking well how are you getting your diabetic medications? Diabetic supplies are very expensive as well. My endocrinologist was taking really good care of me in that department. From time to time, she would set me up with a six month supply of my medication. It got to the point where I couldn't see my physician for medication anymore. I had already accumulated so much back pay for doctor visits and I just didn't have the money to pay. Even though I was working, I still couldn't pay for the visits and the medications without insurance coverage.

When you think you have used up all your options, please believe me when I say that God will make a way out of no way. I started doing some research on physicians in the area and came across a doctor from some referrals from friends and family. I found a new PCP, Primary Care Physician, to take care of me and he was great at it. He really worked with me financially, allowing me to pay whatever I could at the time of a visit so that I could stay on my medications properly. I truly thank him for that.

I continued on my blood pressure medications, as well as, monitoring my diabetes; but yet again, my body was going through a change. I had lowered my stress, salt intake and smoking but deep down I could tell something was out of control, however, I just couldn't put my finger on it. This new feeling started to affect my work habits, my daily routine and so much more.

I had been working at J&F Food Service for 5 years now from 5 am to 1 pm while getting off work and going to class. I started to show up for work later than normal because upon waking up in the mornings, I was so sick to my stomach. Almost every day for months I would make it to work and end up vomiting a few hours after doing some work. I never knew why all this was taking place. I knew I was doing everything right by what my physician had me doing, but this was getting way out of control. This went on for a while and the doctors had no answer for my condition. Test and blood work was being run on a consistent basis in hope to find the problem.

It was things like this that kept me stress. You telling me that you can't find out what is wrong with me after all those tests? My sunshine through this storm would be my baby girl, Diamond Little. She is my reason to fight every day for life. I can't give up and leave her here without a father because that would be selfish of me. I love to be around my baby girl whenever time allows for me to. I do all I can to make sure she has what is needed for her well-being. Her mother and I have had a great relationship in co-parenting and from time to time we don't agree on everything which is normal for people to do. Around the time of my daughter's birthday in December, her mother and I got into a very big disagreement and the ending results were her taking my daughter out of my life. This was a major blow to my life!!! I love my daughter with everything within my soul and now she's gone. This one event would start a dominoes effect in my life. Stress on top of stress on top of more stress!!!

Chapter 7 (2008)

As a new year approached, I seem to get more and sicklier. I knew that having problems with my diabetes is the main source but as for everything else, we (doctors too) could not find the source of my new problem. I'm waking up every morning with stomach sickness and it's getting worse over time. The symptoms are getting worse. Every day it's something new. I am losing focus on my job. My work ethics is not up to my standards. This new sickness is affecting my work to the point where I'm not able to make it to work at my scheduled time. I suppose to come into work for my shift at 5am but I have been late and later and later as time goes on. It gets to the point where I'm called into the office at my job and told that my hours are being cut and that my new shift would be 8am-1pm instead of my 5am-1pm shift. See that's a big change for me because instead of my getting 40 hours a week, I'm now getting 25 hours a week. See here is just one more thing my sickness is trying to control in my life.

The final straw came when I came in one morning for work and became ill. I would then leave and go to the hospital where I spent the next 2 weeks. This is where I first heard the word, creatinine. Finally, we got the diagnosis of what was wrong with me. I was told that my creatinine number was dropping and if it gets to a certain number, I would lose my kidneys. I was told that creatinine is a chemical waste product in the blood that passes through the kidneys to be filtered and eliminated in urine. The chemical waste is a by-product of normal muscle contractions. With my type 1 diabetes along with my high blood pressure, this is just one of the outcomes from this equation that allows this disease to take out one of my organs. I've actually done pretty good to have gone 16 years without anything major happening to my organs. I was now given even stricter rules to follow for my health. The doctors told me that if I lose my kidneys, I would have to start dialysis. Now dialysis is something that I saw my grandfather go through as I was growing up, so I told myself that's not something I want to do.

After being released from the hospital for this last episode, I wanted and tried to go back to work but I eventually lost my job. Things just weren't working out for the company and me with everything that was taking place. I was in a spiral downward drop at this point in my life. No job, lease on the house was about to be up, bills still due and no income coming in to help with all these money problems. I tried to apply for workers comp, but was denied. I applied for unemployment, but again, I was denied. There are various reasons why I was denied for all the help I was looking for but that is neither here nor there. I went to the next best thing I could do and that was to pray. I went months of praying and help from my siblings to help take care of things but it just wasn't enough but my God made a way out of no way. I would later apply for Social Security Disability for help and get approved. This was my blessing that I had been praying for. I couldn't get another job because my doctors hadn't release me to go back to work because over the months my creatinine had dropped to the point where I was on the borderline of kidney failure.

I was still able to finish my spring semester of school but had to drop the entire fall semester due to my being too sick from my diabetes. My diabetes was taking a major turn for the worse while I'm losing my kidneys at the same time. Back to the drawing board we go. I'm starting to fall back into a depression stage again. So much is going on and I just feel like giving up yet again. I don't know what to do or where to turn. The time is here and the doctor is telling me that I'm close to losing my kidneys so before it gets to a critical point, they would like for me to start dialysis. I said no, not going to do it doc....

Chapter 8 (2009)

Out of the 20 years of dealing with my Type 1 Diabetes, 2009 was the year that almost took my life more than on one occasion. As I have fell back into my AC1 being higher than normal and my blood gases always out of whack, my endocrinologist decided to change the type of insulin I was taking. See I've been taking the same type of insulin for the past 17 years and she thought it was time for a change if I'm going to get a true handle on my diabetes.

I went from having to draw up the amount of insulin with a needle and bottle of medicine to use at a certain time within the day to a Flexpen where I just turn the dial to the amount I need. Now 17 years is a long time to be on something or doing something so change will come with some type of problems. I start the new insulin intake and things seem to be going fine. My endocrinologist and I continue to work out the kinks on how much adjusting needs to be done for the proper amount of insulin for my daily routine. Trial and error will take us on a rollercoaster ride we didn't want to be on.

I started to notice a change from the new insulin regimen only at nights into the morning. I would wake up in cold sweats and blood sugar count being low. Now a few factors could play a part in this, 1, I had to take an insulin shot right at bedtime and 2, Maybe I wasn't eating enough to feed the insulin intake. Either way, some dramatic things were on the horizon for my life.

As I would drift away into my slumber at night, I would start to have these dreams that felt so real to me. I felt like most of the time when I was dreaming, it was a feeling of wrestling with people while it felt like I was drowsy and all and couldn't control myself. I would soon find out later that those dreams weren't dreams at all. I was in a semi-coma at those times in which I thought I was dreaming. Since I was still in school, trying to knock down those semesters to get that Business degree, I would have class early in the mornings now since I didn't work anymore. My siblings knew my daily schedule like I did so if I was out of place without letting them know, they could start to search for me.

My 1st near-death experience came when I was supposed to been in class but I wasn't and since my car was still outside the apartment, my sister Candi came looking for me in my room. She peaked into my room and didn't see me and got worried. Now I was there but I had fallen out the bed and was on the side of the bed where visually it was hard to spot me. As she searched for about an hour to find me she came back and notice that I was on the side of the bed unresponsive. After several attempts to wake me and she wasn't successful, she quickly called 911. Paramedics rushed to our apartment to find me unresponsive to their attempts to awake me as well. With me being diabetic, they started with the most common solution they knew to have a starting point and that was to check my blood sugar. After checking my blood sugar count, it was 16 so they quickly started an IV and pushed D50 into my bloodstream. D50 is just a bag of sugar water, like IV fluids that will help raise the blood sugar level quicker. As I start to come back to my full state of mind and all, I was told that I almost slipped into a coma and died. When I was finally able to open my eyes fully, there were firemen, paramedics and my family around me. This was a scary moment for us all but it would not be the last. I ended up having 20+ episodes like this first one that almost took my life away from me. These episodes were life-threatening and I almost died each time.

If my episodes from the low blood sugars weren't enough, my creatinine numbers had dropped to the point where I would need dialysis soon. I was given an appointment to go and see a specialist and they gave me the scope of what was taking place with my health. Basically, the diabetes and high blood pressure had won. I will never forget the day I was called in to get my test results back. The specialist told me that I would need to start dialysis sooner than later and I was given options on the treatment plan that I could choose. As the doctor left the room, I called my mother in tears. This is something that I didn't want to do, ever. After talking to my mom, she gave me the best advice a mother could give her son and that was the decision was mine to make. See she understood everything that I've been through over the years because she has been by my side every step of the way. A mother's love is always unconditionally and true. Once the doctor came back in, I gave him my decision. I told him sorry but I wasn't going to start dialysis treatments no time soon. I guess since it was early on in the diagnosis that the look on his face was shocking but not too shocking. We talked a little while longer about what will take place over the next couple of months and he told me we will revisit this conversation again in the near future because my health is the most important thing.

Chapter 9 (2010)

After months and months of telling the doctors that I wasn't going to start my dialysis treatments, I was called in and given some bad news. I was told that my creatinine had gotten to a critical point and my kidneys were now failing. I would need to start emergency dialysis ASAP or they will give me about 6 months to live. I was 27 years old when I was given this news. First thing came to mind was my daughter. I told myself that I couldn't be this selfish now. I couldn't choose those 6 months and just give my life up, even though all I've been through I thought about it and my daughter was the only thing on my mind. I didn't want her growing up without a father over something stupid on my behalf because I didn't want to have dialysis treatments. I then called my mother and gave her the news. She told me she had been praying that I would change my mind sooner than later to go ahead and start dialysis.

I received this news on a Thursday and was scheduled for emergency surgery the following Monday. I had a simple procedure done in which a Quinton catheter was put in my upper right chest to be used for my treatments. By Tuesday evening, I was getting my very first dialysis treatment but there would be plenty where that came from.

I stayed in the hospital for about a week getting treatments while monitoring my site and how the treatments were going before they let me go to my treatment center. Due to geographic location or where I was living within the city, I was supposed to have gotten a chair at a dialysis center close to my home. Unfortunately all the seats on the schedule were booked so I was sent to a different site in the West part of the city. I ended up at a center where if I had to do it all over again, I would choose the same one. I made some lasting relationships with the nurses and staff at my dialysis center, as well as, other patients that were dealing with the same thing I was. The nursing staff was so patient, kind and helpful with me during my treatments. One thing I learned growing up was that when people take care of you, you take care of them. Since the nurses and staff at my treatment center was taking such good care of me, from time to time I would cook them a meal and bring it out to them to enjoy. We all know by now that cooking is my passion so I truly enjoyed all the compliments and smiles on each and every face that ate the food. When I'm in town on business or just passing through, I make it my business to go by my old dialysis center and see everybody.

Even though I had a good treatment center filled with loving and caring people, my mindset was set to the fact that I never wanted to be doing this in the first place. I have seen what dialysis does to people. It makes them very weak, makes the skin complexion darker and they are sick most of the time during and after their treatment. After going on a regular basis to my appointments. I was getting in the groove of it, but this process never felt right for me. I returned to a state of depression after having to be tied down to a chair 3 times a week for 4 hours a day. I was going to my treatments on Mondays, Wednesdays and Fridays in the evenings which left me no time to take trips or have any type of fun because I would have to be right back by Monday evening. I got tired of being stuck by two thick needles every time I went in. I hated the fact I had to watch how much fluid I was taking in because that was one of the reason for dialysis treatments, for them to pull excess fluid off of you. It was just so much taking place that I got fed up. I started slipping away. I would make some of my treatments and miss others. I would stay on my full treatment at times and other times I would make up anything to get off and go home for that day. I was doing all of this thinking I was bettering myself but, I was actually hurting myself in the long run. It would eventually show because when I would miss consecutive days, I would have so much fluid and waste on my body that it would make me sick.

Things took a turn for the worse towards the end of the year. I kept doing the hit and miss thing with my dialysis treatments and it landed me in the one place I didn't want to be, the hospital. With the extra amount of fluid on me, my diabetes out of control, I was also stressed to the max. I have been stressed for a few years now since my daughter was taken out of my life. I have tried to deal with it the best I could be from time to time it gets to me. I would especially get fired up around my daughter's birthday which is December 9th. I know stress is a killer and with all my problems, this is the last thing I should be doing, but a father's love is true and unconditional. I went into the hospital around Christmas this year (2010) and stayed until New Year's Eve. I would get out the hospital not a 100%, but I was better and able to go home. Once I get home and lie on my bed because I'm still a little fatigue and start to receive these texts to my phone. It was my daughter's mom texting me. She decided to put all our problems behind her and allow me to start back seeing and doing for my daughter. Me getting my daughter back going into a new year allowed me to start off on a brand new journey while leaving the stress behind me. I had been praying for this moment ever since the day she was taken out of my life. Most parents have disagreements about things but it all comes together when both parents put their differences aside and realize that in the end it's all about that child.

Chapter 10 (2011)

At this point in my life, I was on my final leg/breaking point and wanted to quit on life and die. It seemed as if nothing was going my way. Around every corner was another hardship to knock me back down. I've always been a fighter but I think the past 18 years of Type 1 Diabetes, High Blood Pressure, Renal Kidney Failure and now Gastro paresis can break you. I have been thru as much as any one person could stand. Gastro paresis is a stomach condition that allows for you to have acid reflux to the 10th power as well as not being able to digest your food properly. In the normal time it takes a healthy individual to digest their meal, having gastro paresis it will take my food an extra 4-6 hours to digest. At times my food would just sit on my stomach. This is one of the main reasons why I stayed full. I would normally eat one good meal a day and be full the entire day. My nephrologist (kidney doctor) suggested that I eat 6 small meals a day to balance out with my eating regimen for my diabetes. This kept me sick to my stomach more than most. Doctors stated that the lining of my stomach was a bright red from this disease and it kept me away from spicy foods, proper eating and more medications. Gastro paresis took away a lot of the foods I love to cook and eat but my health is more important and I was on the right path of getting and staying healthy. Trying to control this was difficult but when an episode would happen, I would end up in the ER getting Zofran or Phenergan to settle my sickness to my stomach as well as Morphine because the pain could get unbearable. I would have episodes frequently, but I will never forget this one time.

I became ill and ended up in the hospital as usual and at this point everything thing was out of whack. I was still like a lab rat or guinea pig so more experiments were being done on me. I was resting in my hospital bed that Thursday night of my stay and I was having uncontrollable vomiting. The nurses didn't know how to control it. I recall this being the worse episode of my gastro paresis acting up. They called my doctor to get orders on what needed to be done and he told them to try Reglan on me. Reglan treats gastro esophageal reflux disease (GERD). It also treats nausea, vomiting, and heartburn caused by gastro paresis in patients with diabetes. Now this should be prime for me because A) I have diabetes and B) I had all the other symptoms of gastro paresis but come to find out when given this medicine; I found out that I'm allergic to it.

Finding out I was allergic to Reglan was no fun!!! As the medicine went through my body I could feel my neck start to tense up. Next I started to feel really bad muscle spasms in my neck. I was trying to keep my neck straight but the Reglan was making it lock up so while I was pulling upward, the effects of the Reglan was pulling downward and it was WINNING. The pain from this was excruciating. I'm crying because of the pain. The nursing staff doesn't know how to stop it. My nurse Mrs. Pam came in and started to pray over me. Even though at the time it didn't take away my pain, I felt like everything was going to be okay. She prayed and rubbed my neck until the other nurses got more orders from my doctor. The doctor orders came back and the nurses were told to give me some morphine to see if that would help. The morphine actual stopped the pain as Mrs. Pam continued to pray for me and over me afterwards. I know my God and believe in His work.

He has kept me for all this time so my FAITH in Him is real and respected. Mrs. Pam will always hold a special place in my heart for what she did for me that night. Whenever I can, I go and visit her. I've had plenty other episodes with my gastro paresis but to me it was just another trail in the road for me but my God had better in store for me. Remember, I'm a fighter...

I'm still fighting to finish school and get my degree but my episodes of sickness is standing in the way every time. I have been fighting 10 years to receive this degree from the University of Arkansas at Little Rock and right when I get close, my gastro paresis flares up so bad that my sisters have to call my mother in town. I'm about 2 weeks away from walking the stage so my mother would be heading to Little Rock anyway but my getting sick brought her in a little early. I tell my mother that my chest is hurting really really bad and something is wrong. You know us, when something is wrong with me, I take no chances and go straight the ER to get test ran. We actually ended up going to two hospitals that night because the 1st hospital told us that they didn't find anything wrong in my blood work and that I was just having chest pains. They discharged me and sent me home but I told my mother that I promise you something isn't right. From there we left the 1st hospital and went to the 2nd hospital's ER.

We made them aware of everything that took place at the previous hospital but I was still having real bad chest pains. With all my medical history, I was immediately rushed to the back for tests. 45 minutes later the nursing staff rushed into my ER room and told me to drink this liquid that brought in for me. It was a thick, sweet chalky liquid that I needed to drink before my heart burst. Yes, before my heart burst!!! What the 1st hospital missed thank God the 2nd hospital found in my blood work. My potassium was so high I was on the verge of having a massive heart attack. Now for some strange reason with me and my health, once one thing is off everything else is triggered.

As I'm drinking this liquid to help my potassium level decrease, my gastro paresis is all out of control. I start to have those real unbearable pains and uncontrollable vomiting. I was fed up at this point and don't won't to fight anymore. I have endured so much over the years and just thought to myself I can't win. I trust and believe in God but I was ready to go on home to be with him. I asked my mother to call her pastor and ask him a question for me. I wanted to know, if I give up would I still go to heaven? I'm only able to write this book due to the look on my mother's face as I asked her that question and the tears that were rolling down her face. She hated to see my in these type of conditions and I hate to see my mother cry so I stayed in the fight a little longer.

I was eventually admitted to a room and stayed in the hospital about two weeks. My doctor and nursing staff got me back together but I still wasn't at 100%. I would say I was about at 75-80 percent but there was only one problem with that, graduation was Saturday. It took me talking to my doctor for 3 days straight, begging and pleading my case for him to let me out so that I could walk at my college graduation. I begged and begged and begged and Saturday morning, the day of graduation, I was discharged. I wasn't at full strength but my college graduation meant so much to me and he understood that. I was able to make it home a couple hours before the graduates had to be at the university. With me still being weak as I was, I had to sit with my peers during the ceremony while in a wheelchair. When it was time to receive our degrees, I was wheeled to the front but my determination to show the person that was helping me that I wanted and needed to walk across the stage to receive my degree. I was able to make that walk across the stage to receive my Bachelor of Business Administration from the University of Arkansas at Little Rock in May of 2011.

What a blessing it was to be able to finish college even with me dealing with dialysis 3 times a week!!! I had to take some online classes to help complete my degree because a dialysis treatment left me physically exhausted. Dialysis was not my friend and I truly HATED going. After graduation, I was so bad at going to get my treatments that I had missed so much, the center sent a police officer to my home to check on me. I get a knock at the door and when I opened it, there were two police officers standing there. My first reaction was that I'm no troublemaker so why would they be here. They explained to me that my dialysis center couldn't get in touch with me or my family concerning my treatments and they wanted to make sure I was ok. I was totally in the wrong because I was ignoring the calls from my family as well during this time. Having my dialysis treatments was my new lifeline and without them I would die sooner than later. You have to look at it like this; your kidneys clean the toxicants and waste 24 hours a day, 7 days a week from your body but me on the other hand my dialysis treatments gives me only 7.5 hours to 12 hours a week. It doesn't even compare to a full day of cleaning for those on dialysis.

Even after the visit from the police officers and starting to attend all my treatments again, I still wasn't doing right. I was just in a very depressed state of mind. One night after returning from my dialysis treatment, something hit me hard. I went home and just had the longest talk I've ever had with my God. You see while I'm being stubborn and not wanting to do right by life, God has kept me this long. I asked him for forgiveness of my ways and to show me my purpose in life because after 18 years of heartache and pain, I'm still here. I know I've been through a lot and he wouldn't keep me if he didn't have a plan for me so after that talk with my maker, it was time to do right by him as well as myself.

From that point on, you would have thought I was a mad man. I was going to my dialysis treatments on a regular basis. Since I didn't have class or work to go to, I would even go in early when an available chair came open due to somebody not making it to their treatment. I was doing so great with my treatments that my doctor started to reduce my time that I stayed on the machine. I started out doing treatments for 4 hours when I went it but after I started to go on a consistent basis, he cut my time down to 2 hours and 30 minutes. My numbers were looking good when my blood work came back weekly. I wasn't having too many problems from the treatments, a small complication here and there with any treatment but nothing major. I was heading in the right direction and now I was thinking about asking about getting my name on the transplant list. After talking with my doctors about getting on the transplant list, they gave me a list of things that I had to consider and do before I could go in front of the board. My journey to make the transplant list was in motion...

Chapter 11 (2012)

Trying to make the transplant list isn't easy by far. There is a checklist that is a mile long. After looking over everything I almost didn't want to try for the transplant list but I told myself that I love a challenge. Some of the requirements included having a mental state of mind. The transplant committee will not put a patient on the list if they suffer from depression and other mental capabilities. They told me that you have to have a strong mind for this type of procedure and aftermath. Another requirement was to have a support team. This requirement was checked off from day one. I have always had my support team from day with one with my mother, sisters, my brother and so many more to name. I also need to have a clean bill of health sort to speak. They wanted for me to be able to have all and anything that could be wrong with me outside of my diabetes and kidney failure taken care of in order to have the transplant, no infections basically. For that I had to have some work done.

I have known for years that my diabetes had messed up my vision. I have had blood spots in my eyes since 2005 and I was told that I needed laser surgery to correct the issue. Now at the time, I was thinking, no laser surgery for my eyes and having the possibility of going blind. The ironic thing about that was the fact that as I prolonged the laser surgery, and my blood sugar always staying high, I was helping myself on the verge of going blind. Since I wanted my shot at the transplant happening, I made an appointment to see an eye doctor. Over the next couple of months, I would receive laser surgery for the blood spots in my eyes. Just one more thing I can cross off my list to get on the transplant.

I started this journey for a transplant back in November of 2011. I had to 1st pick the city and state for which I would try first to see if they would accept me to begin the process of putting my name on the list. Those cities included Memphis, TN; St. Louis, MO; Dallas, TX and Oklahoma City, OK. The decision to pick the right city and state is determined by the fact that after your transplant, this where you will have to travel to for appointments and follow-up so I chose the closest to me and that was Memphis, TN. Now if I would have gotten turned down by the Transplant Committee there, I would have chosen Dallas, TX being my next closet area. I was accepted by the Memphis Transplant Committee so there's where I started working towards the transplant list.

I'm working my tail off to get everything done right. For months me and my sister Candi was back and forth from Little Rock, AR to Memphis, TN getting tests done as well as anything else they asked of me. In the process I'm still getting my dialysis treatments while getting so much love and support from my nurses at the Dialysis Center. This is the type of support that was needed for me to push through the finish line!!! Checklist is now completed and on April 27, 2012 while in Memphis in front of the board, I was accepted and my name went on the transplant list. I was put on the list to receive a double transplant, a new kidney and new pancreas. What happens next is, I was told that once your name is put on the transplant list for what I needed, it could take up to 4 years to find a match...?

I will never forget that Friday, May 11, 2012. My morning started off on the right foot. I woke up with such a wonderful feeling about that day for some strange reason. I went about my normal routine because it was a day in which I go and get my treatment done. I ate before it was time to leave for dialysis and I still have so much joy in my heart. My dialysis treatment is as perfect as you can get towards perfection. I even make it home from my dialysis treatment and feel like I can still run a marathon. Then my phone rings. It's a 901 number so I know it's somebody from Memphis but who?

Me: Hello

Voice on other end: May I speak with Mr. Quintion Little?

Me: Speaking.

Voice on the other end: Mr. Little I'm calling in regards to let you know we have found a match for you to have your double transplant.

Me: Are you serious? Thank you Jesus!!!

Voice on the other end: We're going to continue to run the test but keep your phone on and be prepared to come to the hospital first thing in the morning.

Me: Will do and thank you so much.

I immediately got off the phone and called my mom to tell her the great news and to be on standby for when I have to head out to Memphis. I would then call my sisters and let them know the good news because they will be my transportation there due to I won't be able to drive myself after surgery. Last, I would call my girlfriend Solicia Coleman and let her know what was happening.

Was this really about to happen for me after 20 years? All of this happened so fast that I didn't have a chance to get people tested to see if they were a possible match. I had 4 sisters, a brother, family, friends and classmates ready to get tested for me but I was called only 2 weeks later after getting my name on the transplant list. Oh well, no turning back now. I have a chance at a somewhat normal life and I'm not about to pass it up.

I'm so anxious and excited that I don't sleep the entire night. At 7'ish the next morning I get my call that I was waiting for and after running all the proper tests, I was a match. I call my sisters, who by the way were up all night, as well, to come get me so we can make our way to Memphis. My mother and my girlfriend get their respected calls as well, and then my sisters and I are headed to Memphis to get me ready for surgery. Memphis here I come!!!

Getting prepared for this surgery was easier than I thought. I think that was because of all the tests and proper procedures taken in the previous months of trying to get my name on the transplant list. I make it to the transplant center and get checked into my room. There my sisters and I wait for what's next while my mother is on her way from Helena, AR to be with me. My mother has NEVER left my side for any of my medical reasons so I knew she wasn't going to sit this one out. A few minutes later my mother and my aunt walks through the door of my room and I was so elated to see them.

The doctor that is going to perform my double transplant comes in and talks to me and my family about the procedure. He states that he wants the family to know how long the procedure will take and to not worry because I was in good hands. While my transplant doctor is speaking with us, a nurse comes in and is ready yet again to take 16 tubes of blood. This is only the second time during this process that I have had that much blood drawn and I didn't like it. Time is drawing near and soon they will send for me to take me to the prep room and start giving me my IV's and medications for surgery. I'm surrounded by my support for this and it meant so much to me. I then call my pastor, who is back in Little Rock, AR and ask him to pray for me. He prays for me and before they start to wheel me off, my mother gathers everybody and we pray again. You can never get to many prayer warriors to pray with you and for you. I kiss all my family and then I'm off...

On May 12, 2012, one day before Mother's Day, I had my double transplant!!! This long fought journey has finally come to an end. The procedure went well without any complications. I was super nervous going into surgery but the doctors said I did fine. Waking up after all the anesthesia had worn off felt like I had been hit by a Mack truck. I was in so much pain. I had never felt this type of pain but I knew it was well worth it. I had put 20 years of heartache and pain behind me. I was finally FREE!! It was late into the night and my family was still there, by my bedside when I awoke. That is such a great feeling to have. I knew they would be there but my joy through all the pain was when I saw that my girlfriend Solicia Coleman was there as well.

At this point in our relationship, we have only been together for a short time but she has seen me through my best and my worst times with my health and still by my side. I've dated women over the past 20 years who said that they loved me but when times got hard with my health, they left. To open my eyes and see her face let me truly know and understand real love. This is a moment within my life that I hold near and dear to my heart. She is my strength and backbone through the last leg of my journey. I truly love the future Mrs. Little, Solicia Coleman.

The next 3 months of my life was pure HELL. My recovery process was terrible. A normal stay for a patient after a transplant is about 7 days top but I stayed in the hospital a little over 2 weeks. I was told that due to me having gastro paresis that it would be an even tougher recovery for me. They didn't lie about that. I literally was vomiting for 9 days straight, day in and day out. That was very painful because I just was cut in the lower midsection of my stomach. I got so bad that the doctor had to order a tube back down my stomach. Now normally they would do this during surgery because the tube has to enter through your nose and go down into your stomach but this was an emergency case. The nurses come in to insert the tube and I really didn't want it but it was needed. This is one of those worse moments in my life but my girlfriend is right there to give support. Now the procedure starts off great. They go in one side of my nose and as I swallow, they push the tube down into my stomach. Somewhere in all of this the tube came out the other side of my nose and as they tried to pull it out the side they inserted it into, it got hung. I had to be taken to the Emergency Room for an X-Ray to see where it was so they could take it out properly. Can you say PAINFUL!!! Upon finding out how to remove it from being stuck, they still had to get it inside of me so here we go again. Fortunately the 2nd time was a charm; they got it in without any problems.

Even though it took me over 2 weeks to get myself together to be able to go home, I did it!!! I had follow ups after follow ups after follow ups. I left the hospital heading back to Little Rock, AR from Memphis, TN and they wanted me back the very next day for an appointment. The next 3 months was going to be a true test but hey I wanted this so I needed to be prepared. I only missed my 1st doctor's appointment because when I got home, I got sick all over again and ended up in the emergency room. My emergency room turned into a week or so in the hospital. Can you just believe the luck I'm having? From one hospital to another one has been my life's journey for the past 20 years. I stayed in the hospital to the point where I missed my appointment to have my staples taken out so they took them out there.

Once I was able to leave the hospital in better shape, I was due for an appointment with my transplant doctors in Memphis. Now I'm normally the driver but in my condition, I had to turn to my siblings to get me to and from my appointments until I was back able to be behind the wheel. My test results weren't looking too good and because of that my transplant team needed me to stay in Memphis for an entire week to keep close watch on me. Now that wouldn't have been a problem except for the fact, I had nobody to stay with for that amount of time in Memphis. The great thing about the love of a good woman is that she will always come through for you when you need her too. My fiancée has family in Memphis and since she was house sitting she asked her aunt if my mother and I could stay at her home that week since I needed to be in Memphis to get those tests done. Her aunt gave the okay and we were able to be in Memphis to see my transplant team when needed. Now this wasn't an easy feat. Since I was only a few weeks out from the major transplant surgery, I ended up once again getting sick. I went in and they saw that the numbers were a little off. For one, I hadn't been drinking enough fluids to flush the new organs. It's kind of hard to drink 100 oz. of water a day after a major surgery like I had. After looking at my test results, they told me that they couldn't truly tell if my organs were working properly. I was given specific instructions to drink as much water as I possibly could over the next few days for my creatinine levels to go down because if not they would have to do a biopsy to check my numbers. Once I was told how a biopsy works, I went into overdrive on drinking water. I drank so much water that I got sick and ended up going to the emergency room for a few hours but in the end it showed that my creatinine levels went down and everything was working properly where they didn't have to do a biopsy on my kidney.

I eventually stayed more than a week in Memphis due to me getting sick multiple times while I was there. My transplant team was able to pull me back together to get me home so I can start living my life again. I can't say the next few months were easy but hey what's a testimony without the test. I endured some tough days and nights on my road to recovery. My mother spent the next 3 months with me in Little Rock to help take care of me and get me back on my feet. She dropped everything she was doing in life to come to my aid for my surgery as well as the next 3 months after. This is why my relationship with my mother is unbreakable, unconditional love, a true blessing!!! I'm a fighter so after my 3 months were up, I was able to send my mother back home and I started getting myself ready for my next big move in life. When you love somebody like I love Solicia Coleman, you do things to make your relationship work. We wanted to be together but lived in two different cities. Before my double transplant, I told her that I couldn't move to the city in which she lived due to all my doctors being in Little Rock and I do my dialysis there but once I have the opportunity to move, I would and so I did. I left Little Rock, AR and moved to Jonesboro, AR to be with my love.

Conclusion
2014

I won't complain

I've had some good days
I've had some hills to climb
I've had some weary days
I've had some weary nights
But when I look around
And think things over
All of my good days
They outweigh my bad days
So I won't complain

I think of this church song when I look back over my life and the experiences I've encountered with my health. In life, you never know the cards you will get dealt but when you get a hand that you don't know how to play, just let God help you play it out. See most things in life that we complain about are simple but we make a bigger deal out of it. Things could be a lot worse for you but instead of complaining all the time, take some time to be thankful for the things you are being blessed with. There will come a time in everyone's life in which they will be put through a test but how you overcome it will depend on you. As you can see, I went through something that most would have truly given up on a long time ago. I had my ups and downs. I had my fights with God but at the end of the day, he knows best.

I hope I have inspired somebody with my story. If my words and experiences have helped or inspired at least one individual, then I have done my job. See I know I can relate to those that have Type 1 Diabetes but could never relate to those that are going through other illnesses. Now what I do know what we have in common is the fact that we have a battle or had a battle to fight every single day with whatever illness a person is facing. We each have a different path to take and some are more difficult than others, but if we just stay the course and endure, day by day things will get better. If you're out there and you're going through something similar or batting your own fights, my words to you is to keep your head up, never give up. Continue to give God the glory and praise. Be thankful for all that you have and continue to press forward. One of my favorite bible verses that gave me my strength through troubling times is, Proverbs 3:5-6 "Trust in the LORD with all your heart and lean not on your own understanding; in all your ways acknowledge him, and he will make your paths straight."

Author Biography

Quintion Little is an entrepreneur at heart and takes on many different hats in the business world. A graduate from the University of Arkansas at Little Rock, Quintion has utilized his Business degree to be the CEO in all endeavors he takes a role in. He has survived multiple near death experiences from dealing with Type 1 Diabetes but now is running a new race in life. After a true blessing from God to receive a double transplant, he is willing to share his life story with the world in his autobiography. A newly published author, this is his 1st book of many more to come. He has a strong passion for cooking and looks forward to writing a cookbook in the near future. He looks forward to becoming a public speaker and traveling all over the world to give his testimony and help change lives. He currently resides in Jonesboro, Arkansas.

www.ingramcontent.com/pod-product-compliance
Ingram Content Group UK Ltd.
Pitfield, Milton Keynes, MK11 3LW, UK
UKHW020239250726
13967UKWH00001B/453